BEFRIENDING
SILENCE

"Drawing on his personal experience and expansive knowledge, Carl McColman skillfully presents readers with an accessible introduction to the beauty of Cistercian spirituality. As the Rule of Benedict instructs, readers will be inspired to 'listen carefully' to the wisdom of a tradition that continues to speak powerfully to women and men. Not only does *Befriending Silence* guide us in the gifts of Cistercian spirituality, but it's also a tremendous gift to all spiritual seekers!"

Rev. Daniel P. Horan, O.F.M.
Author of *The Franciscan Heart of Thomas Merton*

"Carl McColman gives us a gentle, conversational, and humbly persuasive presentation of the spiritual benefits (and joys) of vowed and disciplined association with monastic life and practice for Christian lay folk. Himself a Lay Cistercian, McColman speaks with quiet assurance about our human need to be ever more mindful of, and intentional about, our 'God-hunger' and the holy yearning from which it comes. In doing so, he has added a practical as well as an informing volume to the literature of faith."

Phyllis Tickle
Founding editor of the Religion Department of *Publishers Weekly*

"*Befriending Silence* is a great gift to all who hunger for meaning, mystery, peace, hope, and God. It takes wisdom from an important contemplative tradition and offers it to all. It is beautifully and humbly written; a joy on many levels."

Brian D. McLaren
Speaker and author of *We Make the Road by Walking*

"*Befriending Silence* is useful and stimulating to anyone who wishes to profit from the substantial wisdom of the Cistercian tradition."

Michael Casey, O.C.S.O.
Cistercian monk and author of *Seventy-Four Tools for Good Living*

"It's a pleasure to recommend Carl McColman's new book on Cistercian spirituality, *Befriending Silence*. It manifests in a wonderful way the Cistercian charism which today is shared by Lay Cistercians and also guides mature seekers."

Br. Patrick Hart, O.C.S.O.
Cistercian monk and former secretary to Thomas Merton

BEFRIENDING SILENCE

DISCOVERING THE GIFTS OF CISTERCIAN SPIRITUALITY

CARL McCOLMAN

AVE MARIA PRESS AVE Notre Dame, Indiana

Founded in 1865, Ave Maria Press is a ministry of the United States Province of Holy Cross.

www.avemariapress.com

Paperback: ISBN-13 978-1-59471-615-7

E-book: ISBN-13 978-1-59471-616-4

Cover image @ Le Thoronet Abbey—Cistercian abbey, Provence, France | Fotolia.

Cover by Angela Moody.

Printed and bound in the United States of America.

Library of Congress Cataloging-in-Publication Data is available.

McColman, Carl.

  Befriending silence : discovering the gifts of Cistercian spirituality / Carl McColman.

     pages cm

  Includes bibliographical references.

  ISBN 978-1-59471-615-7 -- ISBN 1-59471-615-3

  1. Cistercians--Spiritual life. 2. Spirituality--Christianity. 3. Spiritual life--Christianity. I. Title.

  BX3403.M33 2015

  248.4'82--dc23

                         2015018827

FOR PACO AND MALIKA,

AND, OF COURSE,

RHIANNON

We did not come here for the scenery, the architecture, the fresh air, the music, the country life, or for human friendship. . . . We were brought here that God's love might live in us.

—Thomas Merton, *The Waters of Siloe*

The persons I know who are most advanced in prayer are married or engaged in active ministries, running around all day to fulfill their duties.

—Thomas Keating, *Open Mind, Open Heart*

CONTENTS

A NOTE ABOUT LANGUAGE

Many men and women over the centuries have given themselves to Cistercian spirituality, a beautiful and inclusive way of contemplative life. Technically speaking, a vowed member of a Cistercian monastery is called a *monk*—regardless of the person's gender. Unless I am specifically referring to men, please bear in mind the word *monks* is meant to be inclusive of both men and women. The common English word for monastic women is *nuns*, from the Italian word for grandmother, *nonna*. I often refer to Cistercians as *monks* or *nuns* to acknowledge this. I also use the adjective monastic as a kind of gender-inclusive word to signify both monastic men and women.

Cistercian communities are properly called monasteries or abbeys, regardless of the gender of the inhabitants. Since Cistercian monasteries are cloistered (enclosed, or set apart from the rest of society), the word cloister functions as a synonym for monastery. The leader of the community is usually called an abbot or an abbess. The nickname Trappist for the Cistercians of the Strict Observance is typically rendered Trappistine when referring to women.

When speaking of God—who, being God, transcends the limitations of human gender—I have tried to use language that is as inclusive as possible, without abusing either the English tongue or theology. I ask my readers' forgiveness if I have unwittingly perpetrated any unhelpful images of the Divine Mystery.

INTRODUCTION

FROM BERNARD'S VALLEY TO MERTON'S MOUNTAIN

Then, broadening out, we found an empty road.
A thousand paces bore us on (and more),
each of us silent, each contemplative.

—Dante Alighieri,
The Divine Comedy, "Purgatorio"

As the first hint of sunlight glowed on the morning of March 27, 1996, the two remaining monks at the Trappist (Cistercian) monastery in Tibhirine, Algeria, debated whether they should ring the church bells to mark the beginning of their daily round of prayer.

At first, the monks debated because they wanted to avoid unduly alarming the villagers by the absence of the daily pealing. They decided it was too risky. If they rang the bells, the insurgents would know that not all the monks had been kidnapped.

Just hours before, members of a paramilitary group—one of many factions involved in the bitter Algerian Civil War—broke into the monastery and rounded up seven of the nine brothers. Most of the monks were French citizens who lived in a war-torn land far from their home. They lived and prayed among their Muslim friends as they conducted the daily rhythm of Cistercian life through prayer, study, farming, and work. It's a way of life that gave the monks meaning and earned the respect of their neighbors. Further, it would provide spiritual strength for the troubles that lay ahead.

The Monastery of Our Lady of Atlas had been established in Algeria in 1932, during the days of French colonial rule. By the 1990s, when civil war threatened to tear the still-young nation apart, the little monastic community, nestled at the edge of the Atlas Mountains, played an important role in the small village of Tibhirine, which had grown up around the abbey.

One elderly monk, who was a physician, operated the only clinic in the region and provided free medical care several days a week. The Cistercians employed several villagers to help operate the monastery, and the monks counted on their neighbors to buy their products at the local market. Perhaps most important of all, Our Lady of Atlas served as a site where regular meetings took place between Christians and Muslims, who engaged in dialogue to foster respect between the faiths.

As the country descended into the chaos of war, it became apparent that foreigners were no longer safe. Terrorist groups killed foreign workers and members of Catholic religious communities. Government officials met with the monks of Tibhirine, urging them to abandon their monastery and move to a safer location in a less war-torn country. However, the monks, keenly aware of the economic and humanitarian role they played in the local community, balked at the idea of moving.

On Christmas Eve 1993, rebels appeared at their door, machine guns in hand. They insisted to speak to the monastery's leader. The abbot, a thin, bespectacled Frenchman in his fifties named Dom Christian de Chergé, walked fearlessly into their presence, and spoke with authority, "No one has ever come with a weapon into this house of peace. Both your religion and mine forbid weapons in places of worship. If you want to talk here, you must leave your gun outside the building. Otherwise, we have to go outside."[1]

Respecting the monk's faith and his commitment to peace, the insurgents stepped outside the gate. They insisted that the doctor, Brother Luc, accompany them back to their camp in the mountains where he would treat one of their wounded comrades. The abbot refused. Brother Luc is elderly, he explained; plus his vows do not permit him to freely travel. He invited the rebels to bring their wounded men to the monastery where Brother Luc would care for them as best he could.

The insurgents then demanded medical supplies, but again the Cistercian said no. He explained that their limited provisions were needed to care for the ordinary people of the village.

Dom Christian noted that this was a holy night for Christians and asked the armed men to leave. They withdrew but warned that they would be back. Shaken but firm in their faith, the monks took refuge within the rich silence of the night to pray, knowing that this was the surest path to peace.

For more than two years the Trappists lived under the threat of the insurgents' warning. Brother Luc would tend to whomever came to him with a medical need, regardless of their political or religious identity. It didn't matter if they were involved in the war or not.

Every day the monks would turn to God, beginning with a vigil in the early hours of the morning, followed by normal monastic rhythm of prayer throughout the day. Although a number of them had their doubts at first about staying in such a dangerous place, they all came to believe that their calling mandated that they stay. After all, the villagers were under the same threat of violence. Why should they exercise the privilege of being foreigners who could afford to move away? Why should they leave behind the neighbors they had grown to care for, people who lacked the freedom to make such a choice?

So they kept being faithful. Brother Luc ran his clinic, and Dom Christian continued his work for interreligious dialogue. At one o'clock on that fateful morning in March 1996, twenty armed guerrillas returned. This time there was no room for negotiation. All of the monks were carried away except for Brothers Jean-Pierre and Amédée, whom the kidnappers missed.

Two months later, the authorities confirmed the death of the seven Trappists. Their killers have never been brought to justice; indeed, the circumstances surrounding their actual deaths remain shrouded in mystery. Jean-Pierre and Amédée relocated to a Trappist monastery in Morocco; Brother Amédée died in 2008, but as of this writing, Brother Jean-Pierre still gets up every day before dawn to begin his daily round of chanted prayers, much as Cistercian monastics have been doing now for more than nine hundred years.

The story of the Tibhirine monks is dramatic—a 2010 French movie about the monks, *Des hommes et des dieux* (*Of Gods and Men*) has been called the best faith-based film ever made—but the Atlas monks themselves probably would have been embarrassed by all the attention their story has received. For Dom Christian and his brothers, they were simply living the life they believed God called them to lead. They never set out to be heroes, let alone martyrs. On the contrary, they were following a centuries-old way of life that has been described as "ordinary, obscure, and laborious."[2]

The Tibhirine monks are heroes because of the way they lived rather than how they died. Their deaths were horrific, and they certainly faced their fate with courage. The beauty, serenity, and spiritual wisdom of their way of life ultimately matters far more than their violent end. They put into practice the central principles of the Christian faith: love God and love your neighbors (as yourself). More than just a generic, feel-good kind of love, the love of these Cistercian monks stood firm in adversity, remained centered during conflict, and proved capable of making real sacrifice.

The brothers were able to love this way not because they had read the right books or attended the right schools; rather, their love blossomed out of an entire way of life devoted to prayer, meditation, silence, simplicity, and compassion. Living in a thoroughly down-to-earth way, the monks of Atlas—like so many other followers of the Cistercian way—manifested a foretaste of heaven in their humble, unassuming lives.

It is my fervent prayer that anyone reading this book will be spared the deadly danger that claimed the lives of the Tibhirine Trappists. We don't have to live in harm's way to experience the turmoil, frantic pace, and stress of modern life. We struggle with noise, financial challenges, lack of time, and a society where too many people feel lonely or overly stressed.

In the midst of our hyperactive society, monasteries—intentional faith communities of men or women who live together with a shared commitment—seem remarkable for their sheer countercultural identity. Our entertainment culture is frenetic; monasteries are peaceful. In the midst of ever-intensifying consumerism, monks embrace a life of voluntary simplicity. In an age marked by cynicism and skepticism, monastics continue to pray, meditate, and trust in God.

By giving themselves to simplicity and continual prayer, Cistercians (like other monks and nuns) embody a down-to-earth way of life that places love before profits, people before things, and God before self-gratification.

For many people, regardless of faith or religious identity, it seems evident that monks and nuns have something valuable, like a hidden jewel, beautiful and precious but inaccessible to most people. Yet, in our time that hidden jewel is becoming more available to everyone who seeks its blessings. Thanks to their commitment to values like hospitality and compassion, Cistercians willingly share their wisdom with those of us who are eager to listen.

The first Cistercian monastery was founded in Cîteaux, France, in 1098. (*Cistercian*, pronounced *sis-TER-shin*—a mouthful of a word—comes from a Latin term meaning "from Cîteaux") The monks of Cîteaux were not trying to start a new religious movement; they were simple Benedictine monks (followers of Saint Benedict and his ancient rule of life) who wanted to follow a spiritual path without compromise.

The idea caught the imagination of medieval Europe and soon hundreds of Cistercian monasteries thrived across the continent. In the seventeenth century, some Cistercian communities embraced a reform spearheaded at the Abbey of La Trappe, France, thereby becoming known as the Trappists. Not all Cistercians adopted the Trappist reform; so today, while all Trappists are Cistercians, not all Cistercians are Trappists. Yet, they all share a common commitment to follow Jesus Christ, observe the precepts in *The Rule of Saint Benedict*, and seek to embody compassion and contemplation in their ordinary ways.

In other words, they value simplicity, humility, prayer, and old-fashioned hard work. Those are the elements that make a Cistercian monastery run—the keys to Cistercian spirituality.

Almost from the beginning, women were part of this movement too, so nuns as well as monks follow this particular path (some Cistercian monks and nuns like to refer to themselves by the gender-inclusive word *monastics*).

For centuries, Cistercian spirituality remained mostly hidden from the world at large, since monastics live a cloistered life, intentionally set apart from the rest of society. Thanks to a new spirit of openness that followed the Second Vatican Council (Vatican II) in the Catholic Church from 1962 to 1965, along with the writings of several well-known Cistercian authors like Thomas Merton, the unique spirituality of the Cistercians has become more accessible than ever.

Still, plenty of questions can arise when we look at the Cistercian world.

- How is it that an intentionally plain and unexciting way of life continues to attract men and women, century after century?
- What are the secret ingredients that make the Cistercian life so compelling?
- What inspired the monks of Tibhirine to remain in harm's way; what gave them the faith, the strength, and the resolve to continue caring for their neighbors, even though eventually most of them gave their lives to do so?

- Can the wisdom, the gifts, and the practices of Cistercian spirituality bless and challenge Christians who live outside monastery walls?

These are some of the questions we'll explore in this book. This is a book I've written largely out of my own experience, for I am a *Lay Cistercian*—someone who, along with a community of like-minded men and women, receives spiritual guidance from the monks or nuns of a sponsoring monastery. In my case, it's the Monastery of the Holy Spirit in Conyers, Georgia. About fifty such lay communities exist around the world, always under the direction of a Cistercian monastery. A relatively new movement, the first formal Lay Cistercian communities were established in the 1980s. It's a movement based on the compelling idea that the practices of the Cistercians can help those outside of their monasteries grow in grace and wisdom. It's a meaningful and rewarding spiritual path; if you think you would like to become a Lay Cistercian yourself, see appendix 2 for more information.

However, this book is for every spiritual seeker, male or female, young or old, Catholic or Protestant, who wants to embody the grace of God, the love of Christ, and the joy of the Holy Spirit. It's for everyone who longs for a spirituality that is humble, caring, centered, prayerful, and contemplative.

In addition to my personal experience praying with and learning from the Cistercians, I drew on centuries of monastic writings, homilies, and history to help unpack the mysteries of the Cistercian way. Fortunately, we have a treasure trove of material to explore. In its formative years especially, the order featured some of the greatest saints, theologians, and mystics of the Christian faith.

One of them, Saint Bernard of Clairvaux, stands among the greatest voices of medieval spirituality. Bernard is one of only thirty-six Catholics to be declared a Doctor of the Church, meaning his writings are considered exemplary for teaching the Christian faith. This puts him in an exclusive club alongside such luminaries as Saint Augustine, Saint Thomas Aquinas, Saint Teresa of Avila, and Saint Thérèse of Lisieux.

Bernard was hardly the only bright light of the first Cistercian centuries. Other figures like Aelred of Rievaulx, Beatrice of Nazareth, William of Saint Thierry, and Gertrude the Great may not be household names, but they nevertheless led prayerful lives to bless us with their written legacy of inspiration.

Cistercian wisdom is not just something from "way back when" either. Thomas Merton, a Trappist monk, was probably the most famous American Catholic author of the twentieth century. Thomas Keating and M. Basil Pennington, renowned for their leadership of the Centering Prayer movement, also come from the Trappist world, along with some lesser known (but wonderful) spiritual writers like Michael Casey, Gail Fitzpatrick, Bernardo Olivera, and Miriam Pollard.

Writing from within the profound silence of the cloister, Cistercian authors weave together devotion and discernment into a tapestry of holiness, love, and the transfiguring presence of the Spirit in their lives. This gives them something powerful to say to everyday Christians like you and me.

In the year 1115 AD, Saint Bernard set out from Cîteaux to establish what would become the third Cistercian monastery in a place called Clairvaux, which is French for "clear valley" or "valley of light." Given the beauty of Bernard's writings, I like to think of Clairvaux as the shining valley. More than eight hundred years later, the American monk Thomas Merton wrote a book that became a surprise bestseller: his memoir, with a title based on Dante's vision of purgatory—*The Seven Storey Mountain*. When it was published in England the title was changed to *Elected Silence*, since it tells the story of how Merton chose the contemplative life. Merton's mountain, it seems, was a mountain of silence.

When we put these two most renowned Cistercians side by side, it's not an accident one is known for a valley, the other for a mountain. Cistercian spirituality encompasses the mountains and valleys of life. It's not just a mountain-top spirituality, emphasizing ecstasy or an experience of God; neither is it just a spirituality of the valley, emphasizing suffering and repentance. It's a way of life that embraces both.

Life is filled with ups, downs, peak experiences, boring seasons, happy times, and periods of grief. We all, sooner or later, shall walk through the valley. By the grace of God, we shall scale the mountain. Life's valleys can shine with the love of God, and the mountain-top can be a place of deep, restful contemplation. Cistercian spirituality helps us to remember these things. My hope is that in the pages to come you will see this for yourself.

When someone chooses to become a monastic, at the rite of solemn profession the abbot or abbess will pose the following question to the candidate: "Whom do you seek?" It's simple, direct, and to the point. To become a Cistercian, you need to be clear about why you are there. The "why" necessarily involves a "who." Whom do you seek?

No one becomes a Cistercian for Saint Bernard of Clairvaux's, Thomas Merton's or Christian de Chergé's sake. The only reason to follow the Cistercian path is to seek God. Cistercian spirituality only makes sense to the extent that it helps us on our journey toward God.

That's true for nuns and monks, who give their entire lives to this ancient way of life. However, this question also applies to anyone who wishes to grow spiritually and who thinks that Cistercian spirituality might teach us a thing or two. Whom do we seek? Can we commit our lives to the quest for God? Can we make a decision to follow Christ, even if the path we follow takes us to a place of danger and sacrifice?

These questions lead to what has been described as "the universal call to holiness." It's a call that comes from God, a call to a life of compassion and service, of self-knowledge and hospitality, of prayer and deep silence. This call, like the questions that invite us into it, point us to the heart of what Cistercian spirituality offers us—a way to seek God.

It promises to be an exciting adventure. I invite you to join me.

QUESTIONS FOR REFLECTION

- Have you ever visited a monastery? If so, what impressed you the most about your visit?
- "Whom do you seek?" If you could pick three or four words to describe your relationship with God, what would they be?
- Most of us will never have to make the ultimate sacrifice like the monks of Tibhirine, but how can we learn to "give everything to God"?

SPIRITUAL PRACTICE: LISTENING TO THE WHISPERS IN YOUR HEART

Here's how *The Rule of Saint Benedict*, the sixth-century guidebook for monks and nuns, begins: "Listen carefully to the master's instructions, and attend to them with the ear of your heart."

Beyond simply listening with our physical ears, the ear of the heart invites us to listen in a hidden, inner way for what the Bible calls "a sound of sheer silence" (1 Kgs 19:12).[3] This verse suggests that God comes to us *in silence*.

"Be still and know that I am God," the voice of God proclaims in Psalm 46:10. But to truly know God in stillness, we need to follow Saint Benedict's advice and *listen*—not only with our physical ears but with the spiritual ears of our heart.

Cistercians, like other contemplative monks and nuns, have always fostered silence in their lives; as Saint Benedict said, "there are times when good words are to be left unsaid out of esteem for silence." Trappists are especially known for their commitment to silence; before Vatican II, Trappist monasteries observed silence so rigorously that the monks used sign language to avoid speaking.

Nowadays, it's permissible for Cistercians to speak, but they still aim to foster exterior silence in order to cultivate interior listening as part of their quest for God. If you would like for Cistercian wisdom to shape your own spiritual path, begin with a simple effort to foster silence in your life. You don't have to take it to an extreme. Give yourself permission to find some time each day, even if only ten or fifteen minutes, for silence. No TV, no Internet, no smartphone. No music or even reading. Simply *be* in silence. At first this can seem disconcerting, for many people find that by making an effort to foster *exterior* silence, they come face-to-face with the noise of their *interior* lives. If that's you, try to be gentle with yourself. Simply offer your interior noisiness—all your distracting thoughts, feelings, and daydreams—to God. Trust that God is present, even if you cannot feel God's presence. "Truly, you are a God who hides himself, O God of Israel, the Savior." (Is 45:15).

If you need to do *something* to occupy your mind during this period of quiet, slowly repeat the following scripture verse: "O God, come to my assistance; O Lord, make haste to help me" (Ps 69:2 DRV). Monastics have been using this passage while praying silently since at least the fifth century. Cistercians, and others, still use this verse every day in their daily prayers. If, however, you find that the verse slips away from your awareness and you are simply resting in pure silence, relax into that: it is a moment of grace. When you get distracted by random thoughts again, simply return to the verse. Let it be your companion in the silence.

You'll notice that this kind of gentle silent prayer may not feel "productive" or like it gets any "results." Good. We live in a world that has turned productivity into an idol. Maybe at the office productivity is king, but when it comes to our relationship with God, we need to learn to let go and simply be. Let God take the lead. Our job is not to tell God what to do, but to listen to God, and for God, with the ear of our heart. Finding time every day for silence helps us, in a wonderful way, to cultivate open-ended listening.

CHAPTER 1

CHARISM:
A GIFT FROM GOD
(WITH A GREEK ACCENT)

The barn swallows swoop through the long stream-
ers of light that flood down from two high windows.
We watch a cat play with a piece of hay. Everybody
is together, resting, in a very simple, elemental
prayer of gift. It's not thought out, reasoned, mea-
sured—it's just gift—God's atmosphere of gift which
we know.

—Mother Agnes Day, O.C.S.O., *Light in the Shoe Shop*

Much of the beauty of the Cistercian tradition resides within
monasteries themselves, as places of silence and refuge. But
just as you don't have to dwell in the Holy Land to follow
Jesus, you don't have to live (or even be) in a monastery to
be blessed by the wisdom of the Cistercians, as a story about
Thomas Merton demonstrates.

Merton was a man who embodied contradiction: a famous
author who was the member of a religious order which prizes
obscurity; a spiritual recluse who became renowned for his
social and political views; a monk who gave his life to God
but whose sins are only too well-known—thanks to the post-
humous publication of his own journals.

A key event in Merton's life took place not in the silence of the cloister but on a bustling street corner in the middle of a city. Like all Trappists, Merton rarely left the abbey, but on occasion he had a good reason to venture into the world. Such an errand brought him to downtown Louisville, Kentucky, in March 1958, when he had been a monk for well over sixteen years. On that late winter day, as he reached a street corner, something amazing happened.

"I was suddenly overwhelmed with the realization that I loved all those people," wrote Merton, referring to the passersby on the street. "It was like waking from a dream of separateness, of spurious self-isolation in a special world, the world of renunciation and supposed holiness."[1]

In other words, Merton suddenly realized that there was no real difference between being a monk (who was celibate and lived in a silent monastery) and being a "normal" person. He marveled over this apparently simple insight, "if only everybody could realize this! But it cannot be explained. There is no way of telling people that they are all walking around shining like the sun."[2]

Without planning it or expecting it, Merton received a kind of mystical vision or insight—what commentators have called his "epiphany." Ordinary people walking down the street seemed to be shining like the sun, and Merton's response was that he fell in love, with each and every one.

In his journal, and later in one of his books, *Conjectures of a Guilty Bystander*, he reflected on this extraordinary moment and realized that it enabled him to see the world in a new light. No longer did he consider monastic life to be a "special calling." He didn't question his vocation as a Trappist and was still a monk ten years later when he died in a freak accident. But because of that event, he began to see that being *human* mattered more than being a monastic.

In other words, the important calling is not the external label we wear but the interior truth of who we are. All people— not just nuns or monks, saints or mystics—are called into a life-transfiguring relationship with God. This insight was a true gift that Merton discerned as a result of his seemingly random sense of falling in love with everyone on a random city street. Why does this story matter? Aside from just being an interesting moment in a great writer's life, Merton's epiphany made a difference in his work. After that day in March 1958, Merton's writing noticeably changed. He became more engaged with the issues of the day, writing not only about pious topics like prayer and meditation but also more practical issues including the political and social controversies of his time.

He went on to revise two of his earlier spiritual books (*Seeds of Contemplation*, revised as *New Seeds of Contemplation*, and *What is Contemplation?*, revised as *The Inner Experience*), seeking to make his writing more relevant to everyone, not just monks or nuns. Merton's epiphany was an important step toward making Cistercian spirituality available to all people who seek a deeper relationship with God.

Not everyone has mind-blowing epiphanies or transfiguring insights like Merton did. But we all receive gifts from God—and it is precisely this fact, that God is by nature giving, that provides an important clue to understanding the secrets of this hidden jewel, the Cistercian path.

I like to joke that my favorite prayer is "Dear Lord, don't worry, I have it all under control!" It's funny because, in fact, I have almost *nothing* under control. The sting of the joke lies in the fact that I *wish* I had everything tightly managed. I suspect that's true for most of us. Whether we have our lives carefully organized or barely restrained, we want things even more orderly than they are, and we secretly fear that everything could descend into chaos at any time. Our finances, our careers, our families, our health—we want to have influence over it all, and we get stressed out when things don't go the way we planned them.

Here's a similar humorous line I often hear repeated in spiritual circles: "The best way to make God laugh is to tell God your plans." It seems that as much as we try to manage every little detail in our affairs, life keeps getting in the way in small and huge ways. A flat tire. Raccoons in the attic. A cancelled flight. A sore throat. A pink slip. A divorce. A cancer diagnosis. Of course, there are happy interruptions too, but sometimes they can be as stressful as the "bad" events. When we face the uncertainties of the future, we must admit we actually have very little under control. We can plan, we can prepare, and it is prudent to do so. But the reason why we say, with Robert Burns in his poem, *To A Mouse*, the best laid plans of mice and men often go awry is because, well, they do.

Cistercian wisdom, in its simple, quiet way, offers an antidote to our near-universal addiction to control. The monks and nuns refer to the character or identity of their spirituality as the *Cistercian Charism*. We'll talk more about this term and what it means later on in this chapter. For now, I want to focus on this notion of *charism*. It comes from a Greek word meaning "gift." The Cistercian way emphasizes *gifts from God* as a central fact of spiritual living. The world tells us that the keys to a good life include power, authority, control, management, ambition, money (lots of it), experiences (the more the better), and, of course, owning lots of stuff. But Cistercian spirituality ignores this way of thinking almost completely.

For Cistercians a good life begins in God. God loves us. Out of that love, God blesses us in big and small ways. The blessings of God are not anything we can control, manage, or earn. They are *gifts*. Sometimes they are obvious gifts: the sheer fact we are alive or a particular talent you might have, such as an excellent singing voice. Sometimes God's gifts come as specific blessings or challenges that help us to grow or trust God more. Likewise, Cistercians recognize God's generosity in many of the qualities that shape their uniquely beautiful, spiritual way of life.

Monasteries are places of quiet and rest, not because monks or nuns are special people but because God has given them the gift of silence. The monastics pray several times every day, not because they are so skilled at time management but because

God has given them the gift of the liturgy (the formal prayers of the monastery, offered several times a day at different "offices" or services). Cistercians are happy, down-to-earth folks not because they have a secret insight into psychological power but simply because God has given them the gift of humility.

On and on it goes. Cistercian spirituality emerges from a recognition of God's blessings, gifts given to us, not because we deserve them but because God loves us so very much. Part of what is lovely about a gift, any gift, is that it can create or celebrate a bond, a connection between the recipient and the giver. On my birthday, when my wife gives me a present, it's not just an obligatory act; rather, it is an expression of the love between us—the bond of love which sustains our relationship every day, not just on the gift-giving days. I hope this is true of all gifts. Even when a salesperson sends a bottle of champagne to an important client, it's meant to strengthen the ties of their relationship—even if it's "strictly business."

What is true on a human level is even more meaningful with the greatest of all relationships: the one between human beings and our creator God. A *spiritual* gift from God reveals how God offers a deeper and more intimate relationship to (and with) us. It points us back to God, the giver.

God's gifts are always freely given. They are not rewards, or incentives, or bargaining chips. We cannot do anything to earn God's love or grace, so we cannot do anything to make God shower us with blessings either.

So what makes something a spiritual gift? Seen with the eyes of love or faith, almost anything could qualify as a gift from God. For starters, the sheer fact that we, or anything else, exist at all is a gift. No one forced God into fashioning the universe or setting into motion the chain of miracles and events that culminated in your and my births. Our very lives, our bodies, our minds, our families, our homes, and our environment—all are gifts, given to us by a loving, providential Creator. From there, we can get more specific.

Each of us has unique abilities, interests, aptitudes, and talents. If you're thinking, "Well, I inherited my talents from my parents and learned my interests from my friends," of course you did—and those people who influenced you and shared their DNA with you were all, ultimately, given to you by God. Christians believe the supreme gift from God is, well, God's very self given to us especially in the person of Jesus Christ and in the ongoing presence of the Holy Spirit in our lives.

Jesus is our light, our compass, our inspiration, our hope. We put our faith in him for the blessings of life and for grace upon our deaths. Even in death, we trust that we can commend ourselves to the heart of God, knowing that as we pass into the silence of eternity, we pass into the safety of God's grace and mercy.

A Greek word for gift is *charisma*, which is related to *charis*, meaning grace or kindness—implied here is a gift lavishly bestowed with no concern for reciprocation, simply a joyful expression of the love of the giver. It's a particularly appropriate word for describing gifts from God. In 1 Corinthians 12:4 (NABRE), which in English reads, "There are different kinds of spiritual gifts but the same Spirit," the original Greek word for "spiritual gifts" is *charisma*. A "charismatic" person is someone with a particular gift, an ability to attract or inspire others. Then there's the charismatic renewal, an ecumenical movement within Christianity that stresses spiritual gifts from the Holy Spirit, such as healing, wisdom, or discernment.

I mentioned how Cistercians describe the spirituality and identity of their way of life as the Cistercian Charism. It's a lovely image. The Cistercian way is entirely a gift, a grace bestowed on those who follow this prayerful way of life. The gifts of Cistercian spirituality encompass a variety of blessings that are available to us with no strings attached. In these gifts we find the wisdom of the past—our innate capacities to grow. They instruct us to live humbly. We are taught how to give and receive love. The people in our lives are also gifts from God, living gifts who share with us their beauty and their challenges. Of course, divine gifts are sometimes explicitly spiritual or religious, so the adventure of prayer, the mystery of silence, and virtues such as faith or perseverance—all are gifts, freely and lavishly bestowed upon us by our merciful, compassionate God.

These gifts, and all the other graces we receive, are meant to help us embody the love of God in our lives. In fact, that may be the best definition of a spiritual gift: any blessing from God, in any form, which helps us to receive, respond to, and share the ultimate gift of God's love.

None of God's gifts are unique to the Cistercian way of life. The blessings that monks and nuns enjoy are available to all who seek divine love. But the Cistercian Charism combines its graces in a distinctive way, marked by the unique beauty and silent simplicity of the monastic life. Think of the Cistercian Charism as the overall character of this particular expression of spirituality, the whole being greater than the sum of its parts. The individual elements of this particular path are the building blocks of a lovely and richly contemplative way of life.

A gift from God is a gift precisely because we do not earn or deserve it. It's free. It's not about our special abilities or worthy performance. God does not parse out the elements of Cistercian spirituality to us based on merit. They are freely available to all, available to anyone who wishes to be blessed by them.

So we do not *earn* God's blessings, but we do have a choice in how we *respond* to them. The Cistercian Charism entails more than just an assortment of blessings. It invites us to put those blessings to work in our lives for the purpose of both personal transfiguration and loving service of others. In other words, Cistercian spirituality includes a *practical* dimension. The action steps we take in response to God's love are spiritual *practices*.

While spiritual *gifts* are blessings freely bestowed on us from God; *practices* are the means by which we accept those gifts and seek to live by their blessings. What does this look like? Let's take silence, for example. The sheer existence of silence is a gift, a blessing from God. To truly appreciate it, however, we need to ensure that we make time for silence in our lives (which is why the exercise at the end of the introduction an important starting point). Anyone can *notice* silence; even secular meditation exercises like mindfulness-based stress reduction invite us to be aware of silence. But when we choose to *pray* in a silent way, we are responding to the gift of silence with a meaningful spiritual practice, a freely embraced way of accepting God's gift.

Remember this. Every gift from God invites us to greater intimacy with God—not as something we achieve or earn but something we may simply accept. The steps we take in response to the gifts we receive are how we say yes to God's love.

Life is a gift, filled with many blessings, large or small, ordinary or extraordinary. The entire Cistercian way of life is a charism, a gift from God. The next time you feel tempted to tell God you have everything under control, take a deep breath and look for the gifts God continually bestows upon you. If you choose to follow the Cistercian path, try to see all of its elements as gifts, given to you by God. I invite you to humbly receive these gifts.

QUESTIONS FOR REFLECTION

- Can you name some of God's blessings or gifts at work in your life? These could be simple or exceptional, material or spiritual in nature. God blesses us in many ways.
- What does *Cistercian Charism* mean to you? Put another way, what does the gift of Cistercian spirituality mean to you?
- Try to think of two or three things (they can be simple, basic) you do to nourish your soul. Would you be comfortable calling these things "spiritual practices"?

SPIRITUAL PRACTICE: FOSTERING A LIFE OF BLESSING AND GRATITUDE

"The LORD bless you and keep you; the LORD make his face to shine upon you, and be gracious to you; the LORD lift up his countenance upon you, and give you peace" (Nm 6:24–26). With these words, Moses blessed the people of Israel, and *blessings* have been a part of religious life ever since. Most churches typically conclude their worship services with the priest or minister blessing the congregation. Many Catholics find great meaning in asking a priest or deacon to bless their rosaries or other religious objects. One of the most common forms of religious observance, even in our highly secularized age, is taking a moment to bless the food we are about to eat.

Human beings have the ability to bless but also to curse. Even if we were imprisoned in chains, that ability could not be taken from us. To bless something is to honor it in the light of God's love. Conversely, to curse something is to withhold our good favor or even to wish for its destruction. Most spiritually minded people see cursing as unhealthy or sinful (especially in the light of Jesus, who instructed us not to curse our enemies but to love them). Blessing, however, is a beautiful expression of care and compassion. For example, we bless those who are in need or who suffer or who struggle to live with dignity and honor even in difficult circumstances. But this ability to bless has implications in our very homes. When we give our children love and attention we bless them. When we do something special for our spouse we bless our marriage. When we strive to overcome a bad habit or cultivate a virtue we are seeking to be a blessing to everyone in our lives.

Closely related to blessing is gratitude: the thanksgiving we express for the blessings we receive. "If the only prayer you say in your whole life is 'thank you' that would suffice," is a nugget of wisdom attributed to the medieval mystic Meister Eckhart. When we express gratitude for a gift we receive, we are actually blessing the person who gave it to us. This is why you find the phrase "Bless the LORD" in scripture (see, for example, Psalm 103). How could I, a mere mortal, bless God? My blessing might be very puny compared to God's gift, but I still can express gratitude. In doing so, I actually offer God a blessing, however lowly it might be.

"We receive the gift of God in vain if we do not use it to seek the glory of God and the benefit of our neighbor," said Baldwin of Forde, a twelfth-century Cistercian monk who became Archbishop of Canterbury. In other words, God's gifts are not meant to be treats for our personal pleasure. They are given to us for the purpose of spreading the love; back to God, and forward to our family, friends, neighbors, and even our enemies (Mt 5:44). One simple way to "seek the glory of God" through the gifts we receive is by the act of blessing.

"Count your blessings (instead of sheep)" is Irving Berlin's advice for insomniacs. That's good advice for all of us and not just when we can't get to sleep. When we take the time to notice the blessings we have received, we can express gratitude—both as a prayer of thanksgiving (blessing) to God and by offering our own blessings to others.

This may seem hardly significant, but it's actually a beautiful spiritual practice. Consider the blessings in your life, no matter how small. Even if your life seems currently marked by much struggle and suffering, look for the blessings between the pain, like grass growing through a crack in the sidewalk. For each blessing in your life, take time to offer a brief prayer of thanksgiving and consider that you are blessing God.

If a blessing comes from a specific person, take time to express gratitude to him or her as well. By doing this every day, you gradually will cultivate in your heart a spirit of gratitude. This in turn will empower you to offer your own blessings to others, so look for ways to do that too. It might be as simple as a friendly smile to a harried postal worker or a gift of fruit to a homeless person near your office. Of course, it could also be a much bigger blessing. But keep in mind that every blessing you give to others begins with gratitude for the blessings you have received. It all goes back to God.

CHAPTER 2

SACRED STORIES: REMEMBERING WHO WE TRULY ARE

If God speaks to us through the Scriptures, surely it
is a matter of some importance that we receive the
message in all its fullness.

—Michael Casey, O.C.S.O., *Sacred Reading*

My father passed away in the winter of 2013, just a few months
shy of his ninetieth birthday. His death marked the end of a
long, excruciating season of forgetting, as dementia slowly
changed the once vigorous pilot and outdoorsman into a tiny
figure curled up fetal-like in a wheelchair. Dad was one of the
lucky ones. His descent into the twilight of cognitive impair-
ment did not erode his basically good-natured personality.
Even in the final months of his life, when no glimmer of recognition would light up his face during my regular visits, he
still managed to keep smiling, relating affably to the nurses and
caregivers who tended to his daily needs. He didn't always
seem to know who I was, but he was always happy to see me.

I remember well the last day he appeared lucid. My
uncle, Dad's younger and only brother, came to Georgia from
Michigan, where they had grown up. My eldest brother and I
accompanied my uncle to the nursing home. The four of us sat

together in Dad's austere room, and Uncle Don immediately began to tell seventy-five-year-old stories from their youth.

The effect seemed miraculous. My father's eyes sparkled, and soon he was fully present in the conversation, answering my uncle's questions and teasing him about various boyhood hijinks. It wasn't a long conversation, maybe half an hour or so before fatigue caused Dad to slump back into his mental fog, but for a luminous moment, two young fellows from the Midwest reminisced and laughed together. It would be the last time my uncle and my father saw one another, and the last time I saw my dad's face shine with clarity. What a precious afternoon it was.

Losing the mental skills we take for granted—our ability to reason, to perform life tasks, and perhaps most precious of all, to remember—seems a terrible fate. "I think, therefore I am," declared Descartes, and to that most of us might add, "When I remember, I remember who I am." But forgetting who we are affects far more than just those who suffer from Alzheimer's disease or some other neurodegenerative disorder. Our society as a whole has forgotten who we are, and the consequences are devastating.

According to the Bible, in the act of creation God said, "Let us make humankind in our image" (Gn 1:26). How would our world be different if we truly knew this, if we believed this, *saw* this: that both individually and collectively, we *knew* we are created in God's image? Perhaps, when Thomas Merton saw the ordinary pedestrians on the city corner walking around "shining like the sun," for a moment he was given the grace of truly seeing the image and likeness of God in action.

But most of us do not see the image of God within us, let alone within others. We do not see ourselves walking around, shining like the sun. We often see one another as threats or as objects of lust or desire. We turn to friends for comfort, to strangers for profit, and to adversaries or competitors so that we can find someone to defeat. We've forgotten that all these people are created in the image of God.

How often do we look at the people in our communities with envy or disdain or simply ignore them, especially the homeless, elderly, or handicapped? We become obsessed with politicians, celebrities, rock stars, or athletes, and then we fly into a rage when someone forgets to use their turn signal. Alas, we have forgotten who we are; we have forgotten that we all are created in the image of God.

Sometimes we see ourselves and one another in terms of a set of descriptive categories. We use terms such as male or female, black or white, straight or gay, attractive or plain, Christian or non-Christian, liberal or conservative, rich or poor. Sometimes, we also mix in qualities such as loving or coldhearted, peaceful or angry, intelligent or dull, charming or awkward, talented or clumsy, spiritual or materialistic, to name just a few. In other words, we are so busy labelling ourselves, judging ourselves, categorizing and interpreting ourselves that we simply lack the time or energy to discover our deepest, truest identity.

"If we look within and examine matters closely, we can notice in ourselves many failures in self-acceptance," notes Trappist author Michael Casey, musing about how we have forgotten the image of God. He goes on to describe how this amnesia affects us: "In our fantasies, for example, we tend to re-create ourselves according to an alternative image and like-ness: unconsciously we desire to be younger and more perfect than we are, without blemish or wrinkle, without any of the liabilities that stem from our genetic endowment and personal history. Without being fully mindful of it, we may be dissatis-fied with what we are. We tend to assume that there is some-thing inherently wrong with us. We think something needs fixing."[1]

Anyone who takes the Bible seriously recognizes that *mem-ory* is a significant, important part of the faith. Consider that mandate at the heart of the Eucharist—in Jesus' words, "Do this in memory of me." Christianity invites us to remember: to recall Jesus, his teachings, and the dramatic circumstances surrounding his death and resurrection and to remember the entire history (*story*) of God's saving actions for his people, from the rainbow after Noah's flood to the promise of a new heaven and a new earth found in the closing pages of the New Testament.

Our faith matters because it invites us to remember our identity. If we have become lost in addiction or despair, faith invites us back to that place where we shine like the sun. If we immerse ourselves in consumerism—the rat race, the endless quest for more entertainment or new experiences—the simple message of Jesus never stops inviting us back to himself. Our faith beckons us back to a place where we remember that God loves us and that God calls us to love one another, to love ourselves, and even to love our enemies (which Jesus taught and Saint Benedict reaffirmed in his *Rule*).

One of the touchstones of religion, and spirituality, is to call us back and beyond. We are invited to go past the ravages of sin, the snares of selfishness, and the judgments of our limited (and limiting) mind. God wants to remind us of the image we were created in—our true story—by helping us see with the eyes of love, feel with the heart of mercy, and think with the mind of compassion.

If you are like me, this call to living the true story does not come easily so we need a lot of help in reorienting ourselves to the image and likeness of God. We need to be reminded of our foundation in the love of God and our identity as bearers of the divine image. The Cistercian way, grounded as it is in the sacred writings of Christianity in general and monasticism in particular, helps us to remember who we truly are.

Once a month, in the crypt beneath the splendid Abbey Church at the Monastery of the Holy Spirit near Atlanta, our Lay Cistercian group gathers for a day of prayer, education, and fellowship. Our *horarium* (schedule) usually begins with Morning Prayer and is followed by the Eucharist. One particular day, Father Anthony Delisi, the monastic advisor to this

Lay Cistercian community, preached a wise sermon about the importance of having a strong spiritual foundation.

Father Anthony has been a monk there since 1948, when he was barely twenty-one (and the monastery itself was only four years old). At the time he entered Cistercian life, the brothers lived in a temporary cloister built of pine board, and before that they lived in a brick barn. For the first twelve years of Father Anthony's life as a Trappist, he worked hard with his fellow monks to construct their permanent home—an impressive monastery and church built atop a massive concrete foundation. Today, the Monastery of the Holy Spirit is as grand as the great old abbeys of Europe, with a lovely sanctuary filled with soaring arches, colorful stained glass and elegant side aisles and transepts.

Although constructed in the 1950s, the church has a timeless quality about it. When the monks gather to chant their daily round of psalms and canticles beginning every morning at four o'clock, a visitor in the cavernous dark nave, resonant with the serene cadence of the monk's voices, could easily imagine that this prayerful place could have been built five, seven, or even nine centuries ago.

Some sixty years after entering Cistercian life, Father Anthony met with the Lay Cistercian community for Mass in the crypt chapel surrounded by enormous concrete columns, which supported the eighty-foot tall, three-thousand-square-foot worship space above it. During that Mass, he preached a sermon in which he told the story of that very building.

"With Advent we look at our beginning, the foundation of who we are," he noted. "We lay a foundation in order to build upon it." He went on to reminisce about the early years of the construction, when the monks had little money and often had no idea how they were going to pay for the building. Working by faith, the brothers balanced their life of prayer with daily work as a construction crew, pouring the concrete with wheelbarrows to slowly raise the building.

It all began by laying a solid foundation. "Indeed this Abbey is built upon a solid foundation," Father Anthony noted. "What the foundations are to this Abbey, so is Advent to the Liturgical Year. We look at the beginning, but always have in view the final end. . . . Jesus became the foundation upon which his body, the Church, is to be built. It is the establishment of the kingdom of God."[2]

The sermon was simple and down-to-earth. Its point—that a good foundation is important not only in construction but in every area of life—applies just as much to spiritual seekers like you and me. Spirituality, like anything else, requires a good foundation. It is our spiritual history and tradition, and the stories that make the tradition come alive, that provide us with a stable and secure base. It is our foundation that helps us remember our identity. Cistercian spirituality, founded in Jesus Christ and the wisdom of the saints, helps us build a house on the rock. The foundation of our remembered identity comes through the stories, teachings, and inspired writings from the Bible down to the present day.

"Those who don't know history are doomed to repeat it," or so goes the dour proverb. Perhaps this can be reframed in a more positive way. Those who do know history, or, at least, the stories that help us remember who they are, can shape their lives with hope. We live in the present, which is always held in a kind of creative tension between the past and the future. Our hopes and our desires pull us into the future even though it's beyond our ability to control.

Likewise, the past gives us knowledge, a sense of identity, and memory of the boundaries that shape our lives. These boundaries separate good from evil, justice from injustice, or behaviors that foster happiness from those that lead to ruin. When we know our history, we reduce the risk of making the same mistakes our forebears did. With a bit of grace, we increase the likelihood of getting at least some things right.

Every Cistercian monastery has a library, and in the middle ages, some of the abbeys found that they quickly collected more books than they had room for. Why so many? Obviously, Christianity is a faith grounded in a sacred book: the Bible. But over the centuries, so many additional writings, filled with insight, encouragement, and devotion, have come along that truly can enrich any spiritual seeker's desire to understand the wisdom of the ages.

Among monks and nuns, one of the greatest of such writings is *The Rule of Saint Benedict,* composed early in the sixth century and designed to help with the practical issues surrounding the administration of a monastic community. But like so many spiritual masterpieces, the *Rule* provides plenty of timeless spiritual instruction along with its down-to-earth information.

Cistercians themselves quickly added their voices to the chorus of great (and humble) Christian writers and teachers. From the first years of the order, Cistercians documented the sermons preached in their churches, the letters of counsel written by abbots and others, and treatises on topics ranging from the love of God to the nature of the soul to the foibles of other (non-Cistercian) abbeys. Of course, monastics also kept, and continue to keep, meticulous records of their business affairs, their membership records, and donations from friends and benefactors. It's all in the service of remembering.

Following the Cistercian path does not mean we have to spend the rest of our lives holed up in a library somewhere, trying to digest the collected writings of Saint Bernard of Clairvaux or Thomas Merton (both of whom composed dozens of books), let alone all the other great Cistercian authors over the centuries. Of course, if you are a bookworm, the possibilities are endless. But the particular gift of Cistercian spirituality that I am calling to your attention in this chapter is not *books* per se but *stories* that help us preserve our memory, just like my uncle's stories helped lift my father out of the fog of dementia to remember who he really was.

First and foremost are the stories (and poetry, wisdom, and instruction) that shape our common faith—those found in the Bible. Sacred scripture is filled with stories, many familiar (Adam and Eve, Noah, Moses, and of course the gospels) and others less well known but nevertheless rich with spiritual insight. *The Rule of Saint Benedict* and the writings of the Cistercians themselves build upon the heritage of biblical stories and wisdom. The stories, poetry, and wisdom of both biblical times and the Christian era not only provide the foundation of Cistercian spirituality but also shape the way Cistercians pray, their understanding of virtues like humility and hospitality, and practical matters like resolving conflict or managing their business affairs.

Reading the Bible or studying *The Rule of Saint Benedict* will not make your problems disappear. Becoming knowledgeable about the nuances of Saint Bernard's theology or Thomas Merton's politics will not earn you any brownie points in heaven (or with your spouse, for that matter). The gift of Christian, Benedictine, and Cistercian wisdom and memory is that these timeless stories and teachings from the past provide the foundation on which we can build our own spiritual identity, our own sense of what it means to respond to God's grace, in our time. The wisdom of the past can inspire us to embrace the love, compassion, forgiveness, mercy, hope, joy, prayer, contemplation, silence, solitude, hard work, and simplicity that characterize a mature spiritual life (in general) and the Cistercian way (in particular). The words and stories found in the Bible, the *Rule*, and the Cistercian classics bless us today because when our lives get topsy-turvy or even out of control, they can remind us who we really are. Such sacred literature keeps us grounded in sacred memory.

Even when our lives are going along beautifully (and we are tempted to pray, "Don't worry, Lord, I've got it all under control!"), the stories and memories of our spiritual heritage can help us to keep things in perspective and to avoid the pitfalls that caused mischief in the past. And maybe in the midst of all this, this foundation of wisdom and insight can help us remain attentive to the main point behind spirituality anyway: seeking the heart of God.

Perhaps most important of all, when we connect with the stories of the great spiritual exemplars of the past we have the opportunity to find our own story within theirs. This is why writers tell stories (just like in this book I've told the stories of the Tibhirine monks, Thomas Merton, and Father Anthony, with more stories to come). When we connect with the wisdom found in stories from the past we gain insight into the issues we are struggling with or themes that characterize the blessings and challenges of our life circumstances here in the present day.

The Bible and other great spiritual writings offer hope for those who suffer, encouragement for those struggling to let go of sin or addiction, knowledge for those hungry to learn more about God, solace for those who grieve or mourn, and challenges for those who are stuck in their own foolish actions. If we approach the Bible, the *Rule*, or other great writings with an open heart and an inquiring mind, the Holy Spirit often will use the words on the page to speak directly to our hearts. In that way, the sacred story truly does become our story as well. I invite you to get to know the Bible, *The Rule of Saint Benedict*, and writings of Cistercian authors, past and present, so that you can find your story in them and remember who you are, someone created in the image of the God who infinitely loves you.

QUESTIONS FOR REFLECTION

- How do you feel about the idea that we are a people who have forgotten our identity (as being formed in the image of a loving God)? What are some ways we can begin the process of remembering?
- Do you have a favorite spiritual book? Why is it so meaningful to you?
- If you were to write a book about your spiritual beliefs and values, what would be the main points in it?

SPIRITUAL PRACTICE: LECTIO DIVINA

Since you can read these words, you enjoy a basic (and, in many parts of the world, essential) life skill: literacy. For many of us who have learned to read and write in our first years of formal education, the privilege of literacy is so much a part of our lives we may forget just how precious a gift it is. We also forget how recently in human history literacy became widespread, at least in some societies.

Just a few generations ago, many people knew only how to make a mark instead of a signature, and reading was a skill belonging only to those who had the financial means to secure an education. Indeed, for centuries monasteries were beacons of literacy in lands where few others would have had access to it.

Even today, the ability to read is a valuable and precious skill. Possessing that skill means having access to the vast storehouse of human knowledge. For many people, reading is strictly a means to an end. They use it to gather information, to increase knowledge, and to expand one's expertise. Some of us read to master a new subject, to understand current events, or to form opinions and strengthen our beliefs. Granted, we also read simply for amusement or entertainment.

But reading can be more than just a tool for fun or understanding. For people of faith, reading can be a doorway not to greater *control* but greater *surrender*, a way to open our minds and hearts to the transfiguring and life-giving Word of God. In chapter 1 I talked about the difference between a gift (something given to us by God to help us grow closer to God) and a practice (anything we do in response to God's gift and grace to open our hearts and souls to God's love at work in our lives).

Just as the Bible is, *The Rule of Saint Benedict* and the writings of the Cistercian tradition are great gifts for us, and so our willingness not only to read these works, but to read them in a prayerful and meditative way, is the practice we can undertake in response. A traditional name for a specifically spiritual approach to reading sacred writings is *lectio divina*, which means "sacred reading."

Although lectio divina originated in monasteries and remains a core spiritual practice for monks and nuns, it is something anyone may learn, practice, and enjoy. By making lectio devina a regular part of your life, you participate in a practice that has nurtured Cistercians and other monastics for centuries. The process of lectio divina is very simple. You choose a book in the Bible to read (many beginners especially enjoy reading the psalms, one of the gospels, or one of the New Testament epistles). Unlike Bible study or other types of informational reading, the goal is *not* to finish reading as quickly as possible. Rather, lectio divina is like spending time with someone special. The purpose is to linger, savoring the time spent together. With lectio divina, your "date" is with God. You open the Bible and read, not to amass information or deepen your skills but simply to open your mind and heart to the word of life that comes from the Holy Spirit.

The first step, *lectio* or reading, starts when you read just a few verses or maybe a paragraph or two. Slowly. Very slowly. If possible, read the passage aloud, for this can help you to read more slowly. As you read, pay attention to see if a word or phrase seems to stand out. That word or phrase may seem to have particular meaning, may elicit a strong emotional reaction, or strike you as meaningful or interesting. *As soon as you encounter this significant word or phrase, stop reading.* If you like, you can go back and reread the passage once or twice more, appreciating the words and allowing yourself to attend to them as consciously as you can.

If no particular word or phrase stands out after you've read half a page or so, go back and reread the passage. Sometimes during the second or third reading that meaningful word will appear. Remember, the purpose of lectio divina is not to gather more information but to seek God's living word for your life.

As you reread your passage once or twice, you may spontaneously begin to ponder the passage's meaning for you. This is the second part of lectio divina, *meditatio* or reflection on the reading. Allow yourself to mull over the words you have read, especially any that stand out to you. This is not the time to get involved in scholarly rumination or study (that has its place but not now).

Remember, lectio divina is not about mastery but about surrender. Ask yourself: What is God saying *to me* in this passage? How is the Living Word reaching out to me through the words on the page? Ponder these questions and seek to pay attention to God's call to you.

After *meditatio*, the third element of lectio divina is *oratio* or prayer—response to the Word of God. Here is where you can prayerfully share with God any thoughts or feelings that have arisen through your reading and reflection. Be honest. Sometimes lectio divina can evoke feelings of resistance, discomfort, embarrassment, or even boredom. The point behind *oratio* is not to impress God with how good and smart you are but simply to share who you are right at this point in time. God loves you and seeks intimacy with you, so share your whole being with God as honestly as you can.

Finally, after reading, reflecting, and responding to the Word of God, it is time to close the bible and simply rest in God's presence (whether you feel that presence or not). This final element of lectio divina, is *contemplatio* or rest. This comes from the Latin word for "gazing," so *contemplatio* (or contemplative prayer) is the act of silently gazing or beholding God, even though God may be beyond our thoughts and imagination. In fact, God *is* beyond your thoughts and imagination, so this restful contemplation is a prayer of gentle but profound silence. Pay attention to the silence between your thoughts and feelings. Rest there, trusting in God's presence.

That's lectio divina. The entire practice might only take ten to twenty minutes. The point is quality, not quantity. Read the Word of God, reflect on its meaning for you, respond to the passage with honesty and vulnerability, and rest in God's gracious silence. See if you can make this a part of your life every day. Like most spiritual practices, lectio divina yields its treasures over time, when tended to faithfully and regularly.

Incidentally, while lectio divina is traditionally used with the Bible, many people find it a useful tool for reading other sacred writings (like the *Rule* or the writings of the saints). The process of reading, reflecting, responding, and resting is such a simple yet beautiful spiritual practice, it can be used with any spiritual book.

But even if you use lectio divina with other books, don't neglect sacred scripture—it truly is the foundation of Christian spirituality and the foundation of remembering who we are: created in the image and likeness of God.

CHAPTER 3

FORMATION:
YOU ARE THE POTTER,
I AM THE CLAY

Yet, O LORD, you are our Father;
we are the clay, and you are our potter;
we are all the work of your hand.

—Isaiah 64:8

I worked for the monks of the Monastery of the Holy Spirit for almost eight years. Hired as a temp one autumn to help install a new computer system, I must have made a good enough impression for the monks to ask me to stay on and produce catalogs for the mail order department. A few years later when that job was outsourced, I took over the responsibility of the book department in the monastery's gift shop. It was a rewarding job, not least because of the opportunity to get to know a number of the brothers as we worked together.

One crisp fall day, when I had been at the job for about a year, Father Anthony (the same monk who preached the "Foundations" sermon) wandered into my office. Stocky and hunched over from years of hard work, this old Trappist sported a mischievous grin and a dry sense of humor that I didn't always get. I liked him but was also just a bit intimidated by his no-nonsense, gruff manner.

"Why don't you become a Lay Cistercian?" he asked me bluntly, not bothering to say hello or trade in small talk.

As a monastery employee, I had gotten to know a number of the Lay Cistercians. They were friends of the community who came to the guesthouse once a month for a day retreat, and who seemed to be in the middle of any volunteer activity needed at the monastery.

While the thought of studying spirituality with the monks in a formal way certainly appealed to me, I also worried that I, a recent midlife convert to Catholicism, lacked the knowledge and the commitment necessary to succeed at such an endeavor.

"I don't know, Father," I said after a long pause. "I don't think I have what it takes to be a Lay Cistercian."

He didn't miss a beat. "What do you mean?" he asked me. "The only requirement is that you're a sinner!" He spoke with a sparkle in his eye, using religious language that has fallen out of fashion but still conveys an important truth: everyone is wounded, is imperfect, is still "under construction."

Utterly taken aback, I stammered, "Well, I think I've got that covered."

On another occasion, one of the brothers spoke with me about how the public sometimes misunderstands the monastery. "People think we become monks because we're holy," he pointed out, "but that's not it at all. We become monks because we're *not*. We need the structure of the cloister to try to become holy. Most of us are weak, and that's why we need the monastery, to help us along our way."

I'm not so sure that monks are any weaker than anyone else, morally or otherwise. I think we all have our wounds and limitations. But what I learned from these conversations with monks is a simple truth that applies to all spiritual seekers: following God—and responding to the universal call to holiness—is a process, not a one-time choice.

In the last chapter we looked at the importance of sacred stories for remembering who we are in God's eyes. Yet the gift of sacred stories is hardly the only important element of

Cistercian identity. Monastics will often say that the way to grasp the Cistercian Charism is simply to live it: to be in community with other Cistercians and to learn by following their examples.

We come to God messy, broken, compromised by selfishness, and wounded by hurts others have inflicted on us or that we've inflicted on ourselves. If we're honest, we can also name the ways we've hurt others as well. By accepting God's grace, we slowly are healed, and we slowly grow into becoming the person God invites us to be. The key word here is *slowly*. The monastic name for this process is *formation*. We are "formed" as members of the mystical Body of Christ, as living embodiments of all the spiritual gifts, including love, humility, compassion, prayer, and silence. In formation, God shapes us into the form of the blessings God bestows upon us. So formation is a means by which we receive God's blessing—and it is in itself a blessing, a gift, from God. Cistercian spirituality invites us to embrace and enter into the formation process, consciously and deliberately.

Eric Schlosser's 2001 book *Fast Food Nation* looks at how the rise of the quick service restaurant industry in America after World War II has impacted so many aspects of our world. He uses the examples of farming, advertising, entertainment, and of course, our health. As our economy has shifted from manufacturing and agriculture to a service/information/entertainment–based system, increasing numbers of us choose to consume quick, inexpensive meals, often picked up (and eaten) while commuting, watching TV, or surfing the Internet. But fast food is only one piece of an intricate puzzle involving how we eat, how we spend time, how we work, and ultimately, how we live. We have forgotten how to be patient. We want results now. We want pleasure now. We want everything now.

Is this a bad thing? Schlosser documents the negative impact that fast food consumption has on our overall well-being, from rising rates of obesity (and subsequent diseases) to the economic implications of this industry which insists that paying its workers low wages is the only way to maintain profits.[1] I mention Schlosser's work not to scapegoat the burger business but rather to point out that "fast food" is symptomatic of our entire way of life—a way of life dominated by a demand for immediate gratification.

Such demand for instant gratification comes with a cost, although often those who demand (and receive) the immediate reward may not be the ones who bear the brunt of the expense. Anyone who has ever felt that their life seems over-stressed or frenzied in its pacing might want to consider that our results— now society may be the cause—and that our entire way of life may need some course-correction. However, such a remedy would by definition take time: to solve the problems of a society obsessed with instant gratification would require a change to a slower-paced way of life.

In the summer of 2014, Lay Cistercians from around the world gathered in Lourdes, France, where they issued a "Statement on the Formation of Lay Cistercians." It says "True formation takes place through an ongoing conversion of life. Our openness to be formed, under the inspiration of the Holy Spirit, is an expression of our desire to embody the Cistercian values."[2] Words like *ongoing, openness,* and *desire* point to a gradual response to the Holy Spirit over time. Clearly, these qualities do not echo the incessant pacing of our gotta-have-it-now society. They emerge from centuries of monastic wisdom, suggesting that God is more interested in long-term, sustainable transfiguration than in short-term, dramatic-but-rootless makeovers.

"We are the clay, and you are our potter," said Isaiah to God (Is 64:8). But how does this happen? What tools does the potter use to form and shape us? For those of us who hunger for the kind of spirituality that Cistercians embody but do not live in a cloister, how can we give ourselves to God's shaping hands?

Spiritually speaking, formation is an interior process, an unhurried evolution by which we gradually allow God to transfigure us, to make us into something new. The "something new" is what Saint Paul called the fruit of the Spirit: love, joy, peace, patience, kindness, generosity, faithfulness, gentleness, and self-control. These aren't just Cistercian values, they are *Godly* values, the values of Jesus.

To assist in their lifelong commitment to formation, Cistercians traditionally have relied on four sources of knowledge and insight to help map out the journey of interior renewal:

- Sacred scripture (especially as encountered through lectio divina)
- *The Rule of Saint Benedict*
- The writings of the great Cistercians
- The Divine Office—the daily prayer of the People of God

The formation statement notes that "by incorporating these elements into our lives, we open ourselves to the transforming grace of the Spirit." As we saw in chapter 2, the Bible, the *Rule*, and the Cistercian heritage tell the story of faith and remind us who we are. No one can digest the knowledge found in these formational books overnight or even in a few years. Truly embodying the wisdom of the ages is a lifelong endeavor, formed through continual prayer, study, reflection, and community participation.

Part of the challenge (but also the joy) of formation is learning to be patient with the process, letting go of the need to have everything done quickly, and instead learning to trust the unfolding development as the Holy Spirit methodically shapes us by grace.

We are the beneficiaries of thousands of years of spiritual yearning and witness. Our dedication to learning the wisdom of the past and applying it to our lives in the present is our gift to the spiritual seekers of the future. In this way, we take our place in the mystical Body of Christ, the Communion of Saints that stretches throughout time and history.

The Divine Office (also called the Daily Office or the Liturgy of the Hours) we'll discuss more closely in chapter 7. Drawn almost entirely from the Bible and from the writings of great saints throughout history, the Divine Office is a compendium of prayer and devotion. It enables followers of Christ to give voice to the stirrings of our hearts and our desire to grow closer to God through worship and praise on a day-to-day basis.

The Divine Office also invites us to discover that prayer, even when offered in solitude, connects us to the community of faith as much as it connects us to God. When we pray, we stand in solidarity with believers all over the world. The Divine Office, by giving shape to our daily prayers in accordance with the faith of our fathers and mothers in the spirit, reminds us of this beautiful truth.

Incidentally, it's called an *office* not in the sense of a room where work takes place but in the sense that these are the official prayers of the faithful, our "work" as children of God, who calls us to offer daily prayer and praise to our Lord.

While the Bible, the *Rule*, the Divine Office, and other spiritual writings help us to discern our formation in God, spiritual development takes more than just reading some ancient writings and saying some formulaic prayers. These resources *support* our formation, but the process itself goes much deeper. It's something that happens in our hearts, not just our eyes or minds. It makes us into new people by slowly and gradually restoring in us, from the inside out, the truth about ourselves which we have forgotten: that we are made in the image and likeness of God. Such restoration truly is the heart of spiritual formation.

Sin has obscured that divine radiance within us; to be formed in the faith of Jesus Christ means consenting, through God's grace, to a process of interior healing and cleansing to restore the image and likeness. It may require years of slowly letting go of selfishness, a sense of entitlement, or a hidden assumption that God exists to serve us rather than the other way around. For some people it may mean letting go of self-contempt, which may have been learned in a religious context. It will require a measure of suffering as we learn to serve rather than to be served, to sacrifice rather than to demand sacrifice, and to put others first rather than insisting on our own ways. Formation is more than just thinking the right thoughts; it is living in a Godly way.

Put simply, through the process of spiritual formation, we seek to be made holy. And in that holiness, we seek union with God.

Perhaps that sounds like an audacious claim. But it is consistent with the wisdom of the Cistercians from the earliest years of the order. Saint Bernard of Clairvaux, for example, "famously spoke about the three kisses suggested in Song of Songs 1:1—the kiss of the feet in penance, the kiss of the hands in virtuous action and the kiss of the mouth of mystical union."[3] In other words, the journey of Christian formation begins with repentance, a new state of mind in which we let go of old behaviors that thwart love and stifle the movement of the Spirit in our lives. From there, we steadily and sustainably replace our old sinful behaviors with new choices, anchored in love, compassion, and other virtues. This process leads us gradually, slowly, eventually to the most intimate of "kisses": the joy that arises from a recognition of God's mysterious and uncontrollable presence in our lives. For some people, that final "kiss" might only happen after death, but to accept the call to Christian formation means to hold this as our destiny, whether we realize it on earth or in heaven. Most saints would caution us that the fullness of joy implied by mystical union can only be fully enjoyed once we have returned to God in the silence of eternity. Even so, by God's grace at least some of that joy may come to us when we persevere.

Formation encompasses growth, conversion of the whole being, healing of wounds, and slow interior transfiguration as we surrender selfishness and seek God's grace to reshape us according to the dictates of love. Although the final fruits of such growth and healing might remain far in the future, at least some characteristics of spiritual maturity and insight will begin to emerge in those who willingly embrace this path.

As we make this journey, we may find that we begin to embrace a spirit of *simplicity*. We seek a more uncluttered life, both on a physical level and perhaps even more crucially in an internal way. We want our minds and hearts to be more open, spacious, and available for the whisper of God's love within us.

Because of this, we can accept austerity, emptiness, and even self-denial as ways to open ourselves more fully to God's grace. The notion of asceticism has fallen out of favor in our day because in the popular mind it is associated with the idea of masochistically chastising or disciplining the body. Images of excessive fasting and of using whips, hair shirts, and cilices spring to our conditioned modern minds.

Even in Saint Benedict's day, monastics could be overzealous in actions intended to chastise themselves. He insisted that anyone wanting to engage in severe penitential actions needed to secure permission from their abbot or abbess. Today, spiritual seekers generally understand that self-denial is never an end in itself and never useful if it is done excessively or to the point of causing harm.

While it is true asceticism can be abused, understood properly it does have a place in the spiritual life. A balanced, healthy asceticism points us toward a greater purpose: self-denial, fasting, or other forms of austerity may open our hearts and minds to be more available to receive (and share with others) God's grace.

Another characteristic of formation is a quality of *ordinariness* about it. As we seek to grow in the love of God, we do not become dramatic in our piety or holiness. On the contrary, holy people typically are humble people (we'll take a closer look at that gift in chapter 4). They are down-to-earth, relaxed, able to work and play well with others, and they simply go about their daily lives in an unremarkable way.

If all this talk about holiness and self-denial and restoring the image of God sounds intimidating to you, please allow yourself to relax. Take a few deep breaths. Remember my conversation with Father Anthony. To start on the process of

Cistercian formation I simply needed to accept that I was a sinner. In other words, I am prone to make mistakes, am anything but perfect, and have my own wounds and compulsions that sometimes (often) get in the way of a healthy expression of love for God, my neighbors, and myself. Just as an alcoholic's road to recovery begins by acknowledging that he or she cannot manage the addiction, so too the process of formation begins with the humbling recognition that we are, in fact, wounded and imperfect and prone to making mistakes. Remember, formation is God's action more than it is ours. Our job is not to make it to happen but rather to allow it to happen.

By accepting the wisdom that comes to us through the Bible, lectio divina, *The Rule of Saint Benedict*, the writings of the Cistercian fathers, and the daily prayers of the Divine Office, we find a wealth of guidance, insight, inspiration, and challenge awaiting us as we seek to let the Holy Spirit form us in his image.

The qualities that shape the Cistercian character can, if we so choose, shape our own character as well. People feel drawn to Cistercian monasteries because they are peaceful, serene, contemplative, silent, and because the monks seem humble, down-to-earth, hardworking, and happy. This lovely, blessed way of life is the fruit of the Cistercian Charism. If we seek to live by the wisdom of the Bible, the *Rule*, the Cistercian saints, and the Divine Office, over time, we will begin to embody some of those same blessings in our own lives as well. It's not magic. It's as simple as keeping a garden. Provide the right soil, sunlight, and nutrients, and your garden will grow by God's grace. Formation in our hearts works the same way.

God is the potter and we are the clay. The Holy Spirit does the forming, and we allow ourselves to be formed. This leads to another characteristic of formation and perhaps one of the most controversial traditional religious concepts: *obedience*. Obedience has fallen out of fashion in today's world because of our cultural assumption that obedience is often linked to the abuse of power. We admire characters, like *Star Trek*'s Captain

Kirk, who seem to make a career out of disobeying orders (and thereby saving the day). We also think of German soldiers obeying their superiors as they gassed innocent Jews to death in the Nazi Holocaust, and we rightly recoil against such misuse of authority and inexcusable submission.

Ours is a cynical age that assumes most people cannot be trusted: Why should obedience be considered a value when it is very possible that the order we are asked to obey is bad? After all—so the reasoning goes—if the Germans had done a better job at disobeying Hitler, the Holocaust might not have happened.

But obedience, at least in a spiritual sense, is *not* about domination or the violation of conscience. After all, if a Nazi soldier refused an order to kill Jews, he would have done so (we hope) because he was actually obeying a higher authority—his innate recognition that genocide is wrong. Obedience does not necessarily mean the same thing as submission to external authority, and the fact that we have confused the two has resulted in a one-sided understanding of obedience that obscures the deeper spiritual meaning. Perhaps our cultural distaste for submission could actually help us understand the purpose of holy obedience: to follow the challenging but life-giving commands of God.

True spiritual obedience is related to the idea of deep *listening*—of *mindfulness* that pays attention to what is right and appropriate, and to respond accordingly. *Obedience* comes from the Latin word for "listening" (compare the words *obedience* and *audience* to see the link). The Holy Spirit calls us to listen to the Word of God at such a level that we allow the Word to shape us, to transfigure us, to heal and renew in us the mark of God's love and character. In short, the deep listening of mindful obedience is the portal to spiritual formation.

True obedience really can only be offered to God. When a monk obeys his superior, a child obeys her parents, or a soldier obeys his officer, these acts of compliance are grounded in a shared commitment to something bigger: to God, to love (or, in the soldier's case, to country). We obey God by making our hearts and minds available to the Holy Spirit that the Spirit might form godly qualities in our lives—qualities such as compassion, mercy, forgiveness, love, peace, and joy.

The *ob-* part of obedience is the kicker; that's the same prefix we find in words like *obstacle* or *obstruction*. It's a reminder that listening to God is sometimes difficult not because God is an obstacle but because *we* tend to get in our own way. "We have met the enemy, and he is us!" declared the old comic-strip character Pogo. We get in our own way, and we get in God's way. So part of spiritual obedience is deep listening to the Word of God, the word of love, forgiveness, and mercy. It involves recognizing that sometimes, and maybe often, we need to set our own biases and prejudices aside. In doing so, we can get out of our own way and get out of God's way, in the hope that maybe some measure of God's love could flow through us.

Formation takes a lifetime, so it's not surprising that it is a theme that will show up again and again in this book. In chapters 9 and 10 we'll take a closer look at formation by considering the vows that Cistercian monks take, including a vow of lifelong conversion.

But for now, I'd like to bring this chapter to a close with this thought: Christian formation is as much about what we let go of as it is about what we embrace. In other words, simplicity, austerity, asceticism, and obedience are all about setting aside anything that clutters up our lives or thwarts us from resting in God's love (or sharing that love with others).

The Sabbath is a perfect expression of this: one day a week we let go of work or unnecessary busyness in order to create space in our lives to rest in God's love and presence (whether felt or unfelt). So one meaningful step on the journey of formation is to remember and observe the Sabbath. Of course that's only one step, since formation is a lifelong process. I invite you to join in on the lifelong adventure, taking small steps in the present to foster a big difference over time.

QUESTIONS FOR REFLECTION

- What words could we use in addition to *obedience* to describe our efforts to allow God to form us?
- In our "immediate gratification" society, what practical steps can we take in order to slow down our expectations for the spiritual life? In other words, how can we make peace with the idea that truly becoming a spiritual or holy person takes time?
- Can you identify possessions, values, beliefs, or attachments in your life that you can let go of in the interest of making yourself available to be transformed by the Holy Spirit?

SPIRITUAL PRACTICE:
REMEMBER THE SABBATH

For several years I lived down the street from an Orthodox Synagogue. I grew to admire my Jewish neighbors who stopped working and driving every Saturday and walked to and from Shul to pray as they marked the day of rest. Jesus criticized the legalism that surrounded Sabbath observance in his day, an obsession with the form rather than the intent that obscured the true meaning of the day of rest: "The Sabbath was made for humankind, and not humankind for the Sabbath" (Mk 2:27).

Christians have sometimes interpreted this to mean that we enjoy a kind of commonsense freedom concerning the idea of the Sabbath. For example, if your job requires you to work on a Sunday, then just make sure you have Saturday off (or vice versa). But I wonder if this kind of Christian liberty regarding the Sabbath hasn't resulted in a tendency, at least in some places, to view the weekly day of rest as a kind of optional observance. In our economy where many jobs now require workers to be available seven days a week, have we allowed our sense of freedom in regard to the Sabbath to turn into freedom *from* the Sabbath?

The Ten Commandments speak clearly on this topic. "Remember the Sabbath day, and keep it holy" is just as important as "you shall not murder" or "you shall not commit adultery" (Ex 20:8, 13–14). The Bible says the Sabbath matters because God himself kept a Sabbath, resting on the seventh day of creation after six days of work.

Here is the spiritual heart of the Sabbath: we remember it and observe it not merely because we don't want to break the rules but because we *do* want to live godly lives. Keeping a day of rest is a way to imitate God, a reminder that work and rest rely on each other. We work in order that we may afford to rest, and we rest in order to replenish our strength.

Sometimes our tendency to forget the Sabbath manifests itself in subtle ways. Maybe we do manage to get a day off from work, but we spend it shopping, surfing the Internet, catching up on our household chores (which have been piling up all week because we spend so much time either working or playing), or managing our finances. Since we're not actually in the office, we figure we're keeping our day of rest. But I wonder if we've missed the point.

I once heard Presbyterian author Wayne Muller (who wrote a book on the topic) say that the Sabbath is all about taking a nap. I think he's on to something. But I also think that Sabbath rest is related to contemplation—prayer founded upon resting in the presence of God. It's a prayer of mindfulness and gentle attentiveness, of letting go of the busyness of our chattering minds and self-conscious feelings. In this, we simply learn *to be*—or as the psalmist said, to "be still and know" God (Ps 46:10).

It's not necessary or even practical to think that an entire day each week should be devoted to religious observance; that idea could lead to its own kind of compulsive legalism. But taking one day a week to be sure you have plenty of time to live at a gentle, relaxed pace fits the idea of a sacred rest. This should include time for lectio divina, going to church, getting in some spiritual reading, enjoying some silence, and then taking a nice long nap. Now that's a Sabbath.

In our increasingly wired world, one way to consider observing your Sabbath is to unplug your technology. For just one day each week, turn off the Internet, your smartphone, your TV, and your MP3 player. Embrace the silence and simplicity of a "technology Sabbath." I'm even tempted to say unplug all your phones, but I know that may not always be practical or loving (for example, if you have an elderly parent who needs to reach you for help). But limiting the use of the telephone to truly important conversations can be a reasonable goal.

Repeatedly Jesus reminds us not to be rigid or legalistic in our Sabbath observance, so I offer these thoughts as an invitation, not a guilt-trip. Here's the bottom line: the Cistercian path invites us to declutter our lives, to gradually pare away all that is not truly helpful, nurturing, or healthy. This includes simplifying how we manage our time. Setting aside one day each week for God, and rest, will yield rich blessings. Try it and see.

CHAPTER 4

HUMILITY: DOWN-TO-EARTH SPIRITUALITY

The playfulness of God is a profound part of reality.
It warns us to not take ourselves too seriously, to
realize that God created us with a certain sense of
humor.
—Thomas Keating O.C.S.O., *Open Mind, Open Heart*

When I told Father Anthony I didn't think I could be a Lay Cistercian, his clever reply was, "The only requirement is that you're a sinner."

Many people, both inside and outside the Church, recoil against the challenging and old-fashioned concept of sin. Most likely, it's because of how Christians have used the word to put other people down. I grew up in a Lutheran church where my pastor, trying to explain the doctrine of original sin, once proclaimed that newborn babies and rapists were equally wicked in the eyes of God.

Many Christians nowadays think it's much more important to focus on our inherent dignity as children of God rather than the so-called depravity that results from sin. Such an emphasis on good news is important. Even so, I am not ready to ditch the traditional language.

Admitting that we are sinners is like the first step in a twelve-step recovery program. It's an important acknowledgment not for the purpose of feeling unworthiness but as a means to seek healing and inner transformation.

Put another way, we human beings are created in the image of God, but we also are messy creatures, prone to choosing thoughts, words, and deeds that hurt ourselves or others. If we want to truly embody the image of God and minimize our capacity for wrongdoing, the first step requires a simple, down-to-earth willingness to admit that we are not God, we are not perfect, and we stand in need of healing and forgiveness. It may be hard to make such an admission. But it is the truth, and for that reason alone, it needs to be acknowledged.

"Believe me as one who has experience," wrote Saint Bernard of Clairvaux to his fellow abbot Henry Murdac, who eventually became the Archbishop of York, "you will find much more among the woods than ever you will among books. Woods and stones will teach you what you can never hear from any master."

It's a remarkable statement, especially coming from someone as learned and as gifted a writer as Bernard. But it's also an important clue to one of the most defining gifts of Cistercian spirituality, or for that matter of any type of spirituality—the gift of humility. Earlier in the same letter, Bernard teased his friend, "If you would grasp Christ, you will do so sooner by following him than by reading of him." Apparently Murdac was putting a lot of effort into studying scripture, and the abbot of Clairvaux wanted to make sure it was more than just an intellectual exercise.

Echoing this idea in his darkly comic novel *The Great Divorce*, C. S. Lewis imagined that a theological society would exist in hell, where great and eminent scholars of religion gathered together to argue pet theories, all oblivious to the fact that none of them had actually accepted the saving love of the God over which they were debating.

Long before either C. S. Lewis or Saint Bernard, Saint Benedict wrote that the key to truly knowing God—to truly living a holy, blessed life—is *humility*. By far the longest chapter in *The Rule of Saint Benedict* is devoted to this one topic. Humility is an essential part of all monastic spirituality and is a key to the Cistercian Charism. It's like a shining light that illuminates a room full of jewels: not only is it brilliant of itself but it is also the light by which all other spiritual gifts shine.

And yet few Christian values have fallen further out of favor in our aggressive, competitive society. The very word seems weak, dysfunctional, or denigrating. Just as *obedience* has become equated with *submission*, so *humility* appears to be the same as *humiliation*, which no one thinks of as a virtue. It's not as if our modern society has rejected all spiritual values. Most people would agree that values like love, compassion, justice, and even forgiveness remain necessary for personal happiness and social order. But humility? That's not something we like to talk about. Or if we do talk about it, it's only to dismiss it as objectionable, old-fashioned, quaint, or even meaningless.

"Isn't humility a form of self-hatred?" we might ask; or equating it with the bad reputation of obedience, "It seems to imply submission to external authority, like the way men have demanded women submit to them, or masters demand it of slaves." We regard humility with mistrust because we suspect the idea has sometimes been used to oppress people or to describe a kind of passivity that may not be particularly praiseworthy. "What's the point of being humble if other people will take advantage of you?" Or so goes conventional common sense.

But Saint Benedict, Saint Bernard, and C. S. Lewis were not in the business of oppressing people or encouraging them to be doormats. On the contrary, they dedicated their lives to helping others finding freedom in Christ. Perhaps there is more to humility than meets the cynical eye.

If humility is *not* about submission to another person or self-abnegation, what is it?

One way to explore humility is through the meaning of
the word itself. We saw in chapter 3 that obedience is related
to listening. Humility in a similar way is related to earthiness.
It comes from the Latin word *humilis*, which literally means
"on the ground." That goes back to *humus*, another Latin word
meaning "earth" or "soil," from which we get the related word
humble. *Humble* also carries a sense of lowliness, whether literally (the earth, after all, is beneath our feet) or socially (a
humble person lacks social standing).

What's interesting here is that while mainstream society
pretty much recoils at the idea of being lowly or powerless,
earthiness has a much better reputation. We admire someone
who is down-to-earth, and most people see value in taking
care of the earth, especially given the number of environmental
challenges the planet faces.

Looking at this tension between lowliness (unpopular) and
earthiness (popular), another thought occurs to me. Perhaps we
might not want to admit it, but we really don't mind humility,
that is, as long as it's somebody else who embodies it. We look
at someone like Blessed Mother Teresa, Pope Francis, or the
Dalai Lama, and we admire them for their humility; but we also
put world-renowned spiritual leaders like that on a pedestal,
maybe as a way to keep them at arm's length.

"I'm not like the pope or a saint, so of course I could never
reach their level of humility." A similar kind of logic can shape
the way outsiders view monks or nuns. "I could never be celibate or get up at four o'clock every morning, so I guess I don't
have what it takes to be a monastic." The problem with this
line of thinking is that it subtly turns humility into something
that it's not. It makes humility into a kind of spiritual sport in
which there are champions (folks like the pope or nuns) and
everybody else (who supposedly lack what it takes to be truly
humble).

But that's not how humility works. We need to beware of
projecting worldly values onto a spiritual virtue. The world
projects onto humility a "win-or-lose" way of seeing things,

where saints or monks represent the "winners" while the rest of us are "losers." But a truly humble person really doesn't worry about who's the best or who's not. Being down-to-earth, such a person usually is oblivious to the fact that he or she embodies humility. And if you point it out, the humble person will smile, maybe laugh, and then just go about their business.

What are some other ways to think about humility—real, down-to-earth humility? Drawing from the wisdom of Saint Benedict and other Cistercian authors, here are a few ideas.

A humble person is an authentic person. Michael Casey calls humility "living in the truth."[1] I once asked Father Anthony if daring to write a book about spirituality meant that I lacked humility. "Are you a good writer?" he asked. "I think so. I hope so," I replied. He said, "If something is true, it's not against humility." But being humble implies more than just accepting our skills and talents. It also means being honest about our limitations, our capacity for making mistakes, and our helplessness and neediness. Sure, such neediness may not be the whole story, but it is definitely part of the story. To pretend otherwise is to step away from being authentic.

A humble person tends to be self-forgetful. I didn't say self-abnegating, self-hating, or self-rejecting. Each of those qualities implies some sort of focus or emphasis on the self. If I am wrapped up in all the ways I think I'm worthless then I'm really paying a lot of attention to myself. Humility is gentler: it neither worships nor rejects the self but rather places its attention elsewhere (on God). I love it when I get lost in work I'm doing, a book I'm reading, or prayer I'm offering to God. Those moments of graced lack-of-self-consciousness are times when my life simply flows without paying too much attention to myself. I'm neither pumping myself up nor am I putting myself down. I'm simply living.

A humble person is ordinary. I've mentioned previously how the Trappists describe their lifestyle as "ordinary, obscure, and laborious." Each of these point to true humility. Obscurity seems to be like self-forgetfulness; it's a tendency to shun the spotlight. Laborious means a commitment to work, including hard work (labor). And ordinary means, well, nothing special. No need to fuss, no need to put on airs. It's easy to see how this takes us back to *humus* or soil. I think it is more than a coincidence that Father Anthony, one of the humblest people I've ever known, has been an enthusiastic gardener throughout his long life.

A humble person has a sense of humor. He or she can see the silly absurdities of life, including an all-important ability not to take yourself too seriously. Humility entails keeping things in perspective, not sweating the small stuff, and letting go of the need to always look in control, dignified, or deserving of respect. Underneath all of our pride and vainglory, most human beings are a little bit goofy. A humble person knows this about him- or herself and is ready to chuckle when things get silly.

A humble person strives to avoid being proud. Pride in this sense means *hubris*, from the Greek word for "spiritual presumption." While there is such a thing as healthy self-esteem (such as taking pride in one's work), pride in its religious sense is a mistake. It's dangerous to assume we don't need God because we think we have our lives under control all by ourselves. Hubris makes us want to puff ourselves up, see ourselves as better than others, and look down on those we see as inferior for whatever reason. But humility represents the spiritually healthy alternative to hubris, calling us to relate to others with compassion and without judgment rather than by always jockeying for the best position.

In a treatise called "On the Steps of Humility and Pride," Saint Bernard placed humility at the foundation of what he called the three steps of truth. "We ascend the first [step of truth] by striving to be humble, the second by compassion, the third in the ecstasy of contemplation."[2] We can take comfort in Saint Bernard's realization that we begin our journey into truth by *striving* to be humble. In other words, most of us find humility to be something we have to learn, and perhaps, even after a lifetime, we will not fully master it.

Trusting in the grace of God, we carry on, seeking to replace our tendency to protect and promote ourselves with an honest, down-to-earth, self-forgetful effort to love—to love our neighbors, which is the second step of truth or compassion, and to love God, which is the third step, the way of contemplation (see chapters 6 and 8 for more on these topics).

As Saint Bernard linked humility with truth, so Michael Casey linked it with happiness: "Humility is a beautiful quality to find in a person. . . . Those who are humble experience no shame. They do not need lies and evasions to inflate their importance in the eyes of their associates, or to buttress their self-esteem. . . . The humble are equally content with both the gifts and the limitations that come from their nature or their personal history. Humility brings with it a fundamental happiness that is able to cope with external difficulties and sorrows."[3]

Jesus himself embodies humility; after all, he said, "Take my yoke upon you, and learn from me; for I am gentle and humble in heart" (Mt 11:29). Casey pointed out, "Growth in humility is powered by the simple desire to become like Christ."[4]

Not only did Jesus embody humility, he also exhibited a related virtue, self-emptying. The Greek word for this is *kenosis*, which appears in Philippians 2:7, when Saint Paul quotes an ancient hymn about Jesus:

who, though he was in the form of God,
did not regard equality with God
as something to be exploited,
but emptied himself,
taking the form of a slave,
being born in human likeness.
And being found in human form,
he humbled himself
and became obedient to the point of death—
even death on a cross.
(Phil 2:6–8)

Jesus *emptied* himself. He stepped out of his powerful position of equality with God, and he embraced earthy humanity when he was born of Mary. This can be an important key to our striving for humility. We can become humble by imitating Jesus, including this emptying quality of *kenosis*. We empty ourselves not of equality with God but rather of hubris, of self-aggrandizement, of our selfish attempts to control, manipulate, or dominate others, rather than exhibiting gentler characteristics such as compassion and vulnerability.

With *kenosis*, we step away from our pride and privilege. We forget ourselves and choose simplicity, lack of control, silence, and emptiness.

In doing so we open our hearts to grace, to divine love, and the whisper of the Holy Spirit. These may seem like abstract words, but they point to a compassionate and vulnerable way of relating to others. *Kenosis* means being honest, even when it is embarrassing or vulnerable to do so. It means being kind and loving, even when it is inconvenient. It means doing the right thing, even when no one is watching. It means turning to God for grace and mercy and then immediately giving that grace and mercy away to others who need it even more. With *kenosis*, we become like baptismal fonts, where the cleansing waters of kindness and compassion are poured into our emptiness from the heart of God, only to splash out of us to bless all those with whom we relate.

This self-emptying is a type of inner decluttering. So often we fill our minds and hearts with thoughts of judgment or competition with others, thoughts of busyness and responsibility, or thoughts of distraction stimulated by our relentless focus on entertainment. Through humility, *kenosis*, God invites us to gently lay those cluttering thoughts and images and feelings aside, seeking instead the interior stillness where we can slow down to listen for the whisper of divine mercy in our hearts.

Our hearts. This is an important point, for pride often seems to be anchored in the endless chatter of our minds. After all, it is the mind that discriminates, that judges, and that continually labels the stuff of our lives—as good or bad, helpful or unhelpful, godly or sinful, fun or boring, nurturing or abusive. Now, the ability to discern is itself a gift from God, but sometimes we use that capacity to judge in unloving ways. We often use judgement to promote ourselves, to condemn others, or to create walls of separation.

But God seeks a deeper truth than the mere black-and-white divisions of our thoughts. God wants to reign in our hearts so that love can be the driving energy that shapes our relationships and our actions. To love, we must live from the heart into an embodied life. Such an embodied life is a down-to-earth life—a humble life.

Humility arises from an open heart and a prayerful mind. It's a quality of character, not something readily learned from a book or a tutorial, such as learning conversational French or how to operate a power saw. Qualities like earthiness, authenticity, self-forgetfulness, a sense of humor, and self-emptying must be learned by example. This is why monks and nuns often will say the best way to learn their way of life is to live it. Humility is more readily caught than taught; the best way to become spiritually humble is to imitate the truly humble people we meet along life's way.

The Benedictine abbess Saint Hildegard of Bingen regarded humility as the "Queen of the Virtues." All the topics we have yet to explore in this book—hospitality, prayer, liturgy, contemplation, and perseverance—are subjects of this queen. We thrive best in a heart made receptive by the grace of humility. That such an unassuming character trait would be so important! Yet, that is the paradoxical, surprising nature of this down-to-earth gift. I invite you to honor the gentle beauty of humility in your own life and to nurture it as the centerpiece of your own spiritual journey.

QUESTIONS FOR REFLECTION

- Think of someone you know (or have known) you consider to be truly humble. Can you describe why you see humility

in his or her personality? Can you think of a concrete step
you could take to imitate his or her virtue in your own life?

- Why do you think our society tends to resist humility? Can
  you think of ways that secular settings, such as corporate
  environments, could benefit from an emphasis on humility?

- Do you agree with Hildegard of Bingen that humility is the
  "Queen of the Virtues"? If so, why? If not, what virtue do
  you consider even more important?

SPIRITUAL PRACTICE:
TENDING A GARDEN

Deciding that you are lower than a worm is not the way to be
humble. As we have seen, putting yourself down may actually
be pride in disguise. Vainglory always wants the spotlight on
itself. "I'm the best. I'm the cutest. I'm the strongest. Look at
me!" If we try to play a game that goes "I'm the worst. I'm the
lousiest. I'm the most worthless," chances are we still want
everyone else to look at us and acknowledge just how *low* we
are. But that's not lowliness, and it's certainly not humility; it's
just pride wearing an upside-down mask.

Rather than deciding you *are* a worm, a far better way to
cultivate your God-given humility is to *connect with* worms by
planting and tending a garden. I know gardening might not be
for everyone, and in the interest of full disclosure, my thumbs
are the opposite of green. But even if you have never raised a
tomato plant or kept a houseplant, consider giving this a try.

Remember that humility comes from the same root word
where we get *humus* or "soil." A humble person is down-to-
earth, does not put on airs, wastes no time trying to impress
anyone but rather goes about his or her business. When we
get our hands dirty by tending a garden or even a houseplant,
we are touching the very stuff that humility is made of: *humus*.

Humility implies a focus on *serving* rather than *being served*.
A humble person tends to like being helpful and pitching in
where needed. Tending a garden means helping the plants

under your care to truly thrive by supplying them with the nutrients they need and making sure they have healthy soil, the right amount of water, appropriate sunlight, and so forth. Even if your long-term goal is to harvest all those lovely tomatoes and fix yourself a delicious salsa, at first you get to take on the humble (down-to-earth) role of serving the plants that will eventually feed you. It's a wonderful *quid pro quo* and a reminder that we human beings are truly dependent on the plants (and animals) we harvest for food.

Even plants we grow just for their ornamental value, like flowers or ferns, give us something (beauty, as well as oxygen) in return for the care we show them. Whether you are a student or a retiree, a cashier or a CEO, it doesn't matter. Tending to the needs of lowly plants is good for your soul.

Gardening has a tendency to be messy. A few hours of working in the yard or the greenhouse will cover you with dirt. Even the much tamer task of tending a potted plant indoors is likely to get some soil under your fingernails. Humility entails a much higher tolerance for sweat, dirt, and grime than pride does. Life is messy after all. Working in the garden helps us to connect or reconnect with the fact that life is all about seasons and rhythm. We work hard, get dirty, clean up, and enjoy the fruit of our labors. Then the round begins again. Humility accepts the cycles of life; it doesn't try to manage or control them.

Finally, tending a garden is a way to participate in God's miracle of life. Every second grader who plants a squash seed in a Dixie cup feels a thrill of wonder when the first green shoot comes poking up through the dark brown soil. We *should* feel a sense of wonder at that. We may plant the seed, water the dirt, and yank away the weeds, but no human being has ever cracked the mystery of life. That's something that belongs to God alone.

When we tend a garden, we do not create life, but we can walk alongside it and learn to appreciate it. We can enjoy the wonder that it brings into our lives. Without the gift of the mystery of life, we would all be doomed, for the food we eat is all (or once was) alive. Plants feed on light, and animals feed on life. All of it comes from God. The low and humble act of tending a garden is a great way to get, or remain, connected to that foundational truth.

If you live in an urban setting or an apartment, growing houseplants or even creating a container garden on your patio or balcony is an option. Look into a community garden in your neighborhood and volunteer to help. It's a great place to meet other down-to-earth people, learn about gardening from a master gardener, and maybe even swap some of your squash for your neighbor's green beans.

CHAPTER 5

HOSPITALITY: WELCOMING CHRIST, WELCOMING OTHERS

All guests who present themselves are to be welcomed as Christ.

—Saint Benedict, *The Rule of Saint Benedict*

For centuries, if you truly wanted to discover the spirituality
of the Cistercians and apply it to your life, you really only had
one option: to live in a monastery.

Part of the nature of a cloistered abbey is that it exists at a
certain remove from the rest of society. Monks and nuns give
themselves to a life where they can be free from *external* distractions so they might be in a position to struggle against the
many internal distractions that prevented them from more fully
beholding the presence and action of the Holy Spirit in their
lives. It is not so much that Cistercians want to deny their spirituality to the Church at large; it's more of a practical matter.
As a spirituality that emphasizes uncompromising devotion to
God, nothing less than a total commitment would do.

But a paradox exists in monastic spirituality, at least among
those who follow *The Rule of Saint Benedict*. Saint Benedict
makes it clear that, as zealous as monastics should be at hiding
themselves away from the unsavory qualities of secular life,

they also need to practice hospitality. They must offer shelter to the traveler, food to the hungry, and welcome to the stranger. The saint even went so far as to insist that guests should be welcomed as if they were Christ himself.

For generations, monasteries have been renowned as wonderful places to go make a retreat or to find rest while far away from home. Even the smallest of abbeys has several guest rooms if not a complete building dedicated to welcoming visitors and wayfarers.

Vatican II brought about many streams of renewal in the life of the Catholic Church, including an invitation to religious orders to revisit their historical roots and look for ways to be faithful to their founders' visions in the postmodern world. For Cistercians, this meant a renewed commitment to qualities from *The Rule of Saint Benedict* such as hospitality—which, as it turned out, proved to be essential for the emergence of the Lay Cistercian movement.

As early as the 1970s, laypersons living near monasteries around the world began to express an interest to learn more about monastic spirituality and the particular gifts of this ancient way of life. In Georgia, for example, individuals asked the Trappists for spiritual guidance, not just on an individual level but even in terms of forming a new type of community of faith. This would allow the monks to mix with married people, priests, and laypeople to form a community that would foster a shared life of prayer, discipleship, and growth in the spirit.

At first, the monks who engaged in conversations like this thought if such a thing could happen, it would have to be in the future. But they listened, and they engaged in conversation with those who brought the questions. Things move slowly in the monastic world, but by 1987 five laypersons were meeting with the monks regularly and beginning to explore how monastic spirituality could be adapted to the realities of secular life.

Meanwhile, on another continent, a similar movement was afoot. In Awhum, Nigeria, a monastery that had been formed as an independent community in 1970 petitioned to join the Cistercian Order of the Strict Observance. When Trappist monks arrived in the late '70s to guide this new community, they discovered that a group of laypeople would gather once a month at the abbey for prayer and religious instruction. While this was not a normal Cistercian practice, it hardly seemed right to turn these devout believers away. After all, the brothers in Awhum were offering these folks hospitality.

Unbeknownst to the communities forming in America and Africa, a similar association of laypersons formed under the auspices of the Abbey of Cîteaux, the mother house of the entire order. Taking Saint Bernard as their patron, the group met in a grange (farmhouse) that once belonged to Clairvaux, the monastery established by Saint Bernard in 1115.

These are just three examples. Similar communities of laypeople, seeking spiritual wisdom and guidance from Cistercian nuns and monks, began to form near monasteries all around the world. By 2002, the General Chapter of the worldwide Cistercian order acknowledged this lay movement, the Lay Cistercians, as part of the Cistercian family. As one woman, who was among the five laypersons meeting at Holy Spirit Abbey in 1987, said, "This was a movement of the Holy Spirit."

But for such a movement to happen, it required the hospitality of the monastics, who were willing to welcome outsiders to become their students, their prayer-partners, and their friends.

◆ ◆ ◆

Hospitality. Usually when that word gets used in ordinary conversation, it either refers to families welcoming guests into their homes or businesses such as restaurants and hotels providing food and lodging to their customer "guests." Because monasteries are now such a marginal part of our society, many people forget (or never knew) how important hospitality has historically been in the lives of monks and nuns, let alone that it's still a central part of monastic identity. Hospitality forges the link between humility and compassion (Saint Bernard's first two steps toward truth).

"All guests who present themselves are to be welcomed as Christ," bluntly declares *The Rule of Saint Benedict*. This is a strong statement about hospitality, particularly since Saint Benedict was writing for those who seek a secluded life of prayer. Such seclusion, as beautiful and vital as it may be, cannot come at the expense of relating to others, especially those who come to the monastery seeking renewal. Monastic spirituality is built around a gesture of welcoming. Visitors are not an interruption, an intrusion, or a distraction. They are an opportunity to directly serve Christ himself, embodied in the person who comes seeking a warm meal or a safe place to sleep. This principle has guided monasteries from Benedict's day to our own, leading many abbeys to set up guest quarters, a retreat house, or hermitages where such hospitality can be generously shared with whoever comes to call.

Spiritually speaking, this emphasis on hospitality carries implications far beyond the basic act of providing food and shelter for guests. Hospitality manifests a spiritual quality of "welcoming" that applies not only to literal reception of guests but any kind of spiritual gesture in which we welcome others into our lives (including God, whom we "welcome" when we open our hearts to his guidance). Hospitality puts people first, finds joy in relationships, and recognizes how the most simple of everyday actions—such as sharing a meal, taking a nap, or resting after a long day of work or travel—all provide opportunities where we can meet and serve Christ in others, and perhaps even bring the love of Christ to others as well.

The traditional patron saints of hospitality are Saint Julian the Hospitaller and Saint Meinrad. Another possible patron saint of hospitality would be Zacchaeus, the repentant tax collector who appears in the Gospel of Luke. When Jesus arrived in the city of Jericho, Zacchaeus climbed a tree to see him. Jesus scandalized the crowd by announcing he would be staying at Zacchaeus's house, and the publican welcomed him gladly.

Then he promised to correct his wrongs by giving half his wealth to the poor, making reparations to those he cheated. Jesus proclaimed that salvation had come to Zacchaeus's house: "For the Son of Man came to seek out and to save the lost" (Lk 19:10). Zacchaeus did not set out to have Jesus come to his home. Jesus invited himself over. Sometimes welcoming others, not only literally into our homes but spiritually into our lives and hearts, is not something we have control over. That does not let us off the hook for hospitality. Like Zacchaeus, we may not necessarily be the ideal hosts. We have made mistakes, hurt other people, and might even have a bad reputation. But that doesn't stop Jesus from inviting himself into our hearts.

So how can we prepare ourselves to welcome him?

Once we welcome Jesus into our lives, we find that he comes to us through other people. It's one thing to offer Jesus hospitality in the safe arena of our imagination. It's something else entirely to have to welcome flesh-and-blood strangers, real people who come to us with needs—whether physical needs like hunger or fatigue, spiritual needs like loneliness or grief, or some combination of the two. Hospitality always costs the person who does the welcoming. It takes time to serve others, money to buy and prepare food, and resources to make a safe home with a warm bed.

But hospitality isn't just about providing a meal and shelter to those who travel. Remember the story about the laypeople in Nigeria? As a spiritual virtue, hospitality encompasses all the ways in which we open our hearts to other people, even if they never dine at our table or sleep in our guest rooms.

For monks and nuns, providing room and board is probably the easy part. The challenging aspect of hospitality is being flexible with all the ways that guests take up time, interrupt routines, and seek spiritual direction or even just a listening ear. To practice hospitality effectively, the host has to practice kindness toward the guests.

When my wife and I got married, we went to the mountains for our honeymoon. We stayed at a lovely bed and breakfast just outside of town. The B and B was in a beautiful home, exquisitely furnished, and ideally located. But the couple who owned the establishment made the experience far less enjoyable. The entire time of our stay, they complained about inconsiderate, messy, and inconvenient guests. Perhaps we got on their bad side because we arrived after dinner, rather than during the expected afternoon hours, and they had something else they wanted to do that evening. The day we left, they hovered around us, clearly nervous that we might try to sneak out without paying (I know we were young, but I don't think we looked like scofflaws). Needless to say, we resolved never to return to that B and B, and later learned the establishment did not stay in business long. Even when hospitality involves the exchange of money, it still requires a basic kindness at its root. Without that, the so-called hospitality is not very hospitable at all.

Monastic hospitality encompasses this broader sense of "welcoming"—not just entertaining guests but receiving all who seek the kindness of our hearts or the attention of our eyes. Directly related to the gift of humility, hospitality requires us to be down-to-earth, authentic, self-forgetful, and vulnerable to truly welcome others into our lives. To be hospitable, we set aside our desires to be special or important. Hospitality means putting the needs and concerns of our guests first. When we welcome others (into our homes or into our hearts), we emphasize how *they* are important, special, or worthy. Hospitality means being so focused on meeting the needs of others that we let go of anxiety about our own wants, trusting that our needs will be met in God's time.

Toward the end of the *Rule*, Saint Benedict devotes a chapter to what he calls "the good zeal of monks." This is almost like a friendly competition: each monk or nun, Benedict suggests, "should each try to be the first to show respect to the other." But it's about more than just being at the head of the line. Good zeal involves patience, especially toward another's weakness or misbehavior; humility (putting the other person's needs ahead of his own); love; and respect. Benedict completes the chapter by saying "Let them prefer nothing whatever to Christ, and may he bring us all together to everlasting life."

Good zeal applies not just to monastics but to all who open their hearts to the way of hospitality, those who make the effort to relate to others with patience, respect, kindness, and love. After all, God invites us to welcome guests with the same enthusiasm with which Zacchaeus welcomed Christ himself. None of us are perfect, and sometimes we can't be as unconditionally loving as we think Christ might want. But rather than be a cause for despair, our limitations can be a cause for discernment as we reflect on how, moving forward, we can gently but intentionally seek to be more and more Christlike in the ways we invite others into our lives.

Any discussion of hospitality also needs a word about being a *guest*—accepting the hospitality of others, especially if we stay in abbey guesthouses. The monks' or nuns' hospitality is a beautiful thing, and we who are drawn to monastic communities and who are invited into their lives, even as guests, are truly blessed. Monastic hospitality can be a source for spiritual rest and renewal, and can even result in meaningful relationships over time, as we get to know the monks or nuns who welcome us.

But as guests, it's also important to bring a spirit of respect and consideration to the monasteries we visit. Nuns and monks are human beings, after all, with needs and concerns of their own. While we can imagine that God's hospitality and love for us and for all people is unconditional, we know that real people have to set real boundaries in order to take good care of themselves. No one can allow guests into their home indefinitely and without limits. The same holds true for monastics.

Sometimes, guests who come to monasteries come because they are lonely, grieving, or struggling with addiction or some other spiritual concern. Monks can be amicable hosts and even offer gentle advice. But they are not our therapists, doctors, professional helpers, or even our pastors. The priests or ministers of our local church fulfill that role. Visitors to monasteries need to remember the first priority of monks and nuns is always to God and then to the needs of their fellow monastics. Prayer and silence come first, and only after that can monks *sometimes* fill a role of spiritual companion, teacher, or friend. "If teaching had become inseparable from Trappist monasteries, it would have meant a change in the very essence of the Cistercian vocation," wrote Thomas Merton, and the same could be said of other roles beside that of teacher, such as spiritual director or confessor.[1] Naturally, individual monks might have gifted abilities to teach, be a spiritual companion, or offer friendship to guests of the abbey, but such a relationship is always a grace.

When visiting monasteries, here are some additional points to bear in mind:

- Do not enter the cloister areas (which are off-limits to non-monastics).
- Do not expect the monks or nuns to break rules for you (such as visiting with you during the great silence from evening through to the next morning).
- Respect the fact that as a guest, you are not a member of the monastic community and therefore may only have a polite but formal interaction with the monks or nuns you meet.

By honoring these boundaries, you are repaying hospitality with respect.

Earlier in this chapter I suggested that hospitality, as a gift from God, forms the bridge between humility and compassion, which is the means by which we love our neighbors as ourselves. The gesture of welcoming is the key to crossing that bridge. Through the self-emptying grace of humility, we create the space in our hearts to welcome others. Hospitality is the act of making that heart-space available to those whom God sends our way. I invite you to cultivate a spirit of welcoming hospitality in your life, welcoming others as a way to welcome God.

QUESTIONS FOR REFLECTION

- What do you think is the relationship between hospitality and love? How is hospitality an expression of love?
- Can you think of other stories in the Bible besides Zacchaeus's that give us insight into Godly hospitality? How about a story of hospitality from your own life?
- Is there an action step you can take to cultivate a richer spirit of hospitality and welcoming in your life? It can be something small. This could be hospitality in your home or hospitality in your heart, such as giving time and attention to those who are lonely.

SPIRITUAL PRACTICE: HELPING SOMEONE IN NEED

Then the king will say to those at his right hand, "Come, you that are blessed by my Father, inherit the kingdom prepared for you from the foundation of the world; for I was hungry and you gave me food, I was thirsty and you gave me something to drink, I was a stranger and you welcomed me, I was naked and you gave me clothing, I was sick and you took care of me, I was in prison and you visited me." Then the righteous will answer him, "Lord, when was it that we saw you hungry and gave you food, or thirsty and gave you something to drink? And when was it that we saw you a stranger and welcomed you, or naked and gave you clothing? And when was it that we saw you sick or in prison and visited you?" And the king will answer them, "Truly I tell you, just as you did it to one of the least of these who are members of my family, you did it to me." (Mt 25:34–40)

Saint Benedict's mandate that monks should welcome guests as if they were Christ clearly has its roots in this parable of the last judgment. Jesus praises his followers for feeding him, welcoming him, and visiting him. When they question him, he points out that by offering such kindnesses to those who were in need, they were in fact ministering to him as well.

When we seek to follow Jesus more closely, this may seem to be a daunting task, but even the most simple or modest act of kindness given to someone in need is a response to the challenge of Matthew 25. Even though most of our efforts to help others will take place not in our homes but in the community, this still qualifies as an act of hospitality since we are welcoming those in need into our hearts, even if only for a short time as we seek to help them out.

Unfortunately, it is far too easy to find someone in need. Soup kitchens and homeless shelters are often strained beyond the limits of their resources. Too many in nursing homes and assisted living centers struggle with loneliness, their families too far away or too busy to visit. Prisons, likewise, house countless inmates who seek to better their lives and who hunger for guidance in the way of following Jesus Christ.

Nobody can do it all. Each of us, in seeking to respond to the mandate to welcome or serve others as Christ, must find the appropriate way to open our hearts. This is not a call to martyrdom. We have to balance our care for others with the right amount of care for ourselves and our loved ones, which means setting appropriate limits. But hospitality is about being open and generous, so sometimes we have to push against the very limits we set.

Monks and nuns often provide excellent examples for how best to serve those in need. At the Monastery of the Holy Spirit, a weekly food bank offers supplies to hundreds of local families in need. But it only operates one day a week, and the social services that make referrals are instructed to let people know what day they can come to seek the food they need. Hospitality is like a gate in a fence: the gate is necessary to allow people in or out of the boundary, but the boundary is still there, and it serves a necessary function.

Sometimes, a person in need is very close to home: a family member who is having difficulty finding work, an elderly aunt grieving the loss of her lifelong spouse, or the neighbor whose son is struggling with his high school geometry homework.

To help those in need, we don't always have to volunteer at a local nonprofit. We just need to answer the call to be a good neighbor or an attentive relative.

But this is not to dismiss charitable work. Sometimes the most important thing we can do is step outside our comfort zones, and volunteering to help others can be a meaningful way to do that. We might begin with our natural talents. If you like to cook, volunteer to prepare a meal at a local homeless shelter. If you're a natural teacher, look for a literacy program where you can help an adult learn to read and write. But whatever you do, look for opportunities to connect with the person (or people) you are helping. Caring gestures such as eye contact, a friendly smile, and a brief conversation may very well matter more to a hungry person than a sack with a sandwich and a cup of hot soup.

Only you can decide how much time you make available to those who are in need. There's no magic formula here; some people give multiple hours every week, while others might have to limit such activities to just an occasional evening or weekend. Like everything else in the spiritual life, it's the relationship that matters, not the appointment book. If you don't already have a way in your life to help others, pray for such an opportunity to come your way (and mention it to your priest or minister). You will probably soon discover that the person who is most blessed by your hospitality to those in need is you yourself.

CHAPTER 6

COMPASSION AND COMMUNITY: WHERE TWO OR THREE ARE GATHERED

It is in communion, even when this proves painful, that a charism is seen to be authentic and mysteriously fruitful.

—Pope Francis, *Evangelii Gaudium*

Like many people, when I first visited a monastery I had all sorts of romantic notions about monastic life. Growing up a Lutheran in the American South, I did not have any exposure to monks or nuns until I was an adult, and my first glimpse into the world of the cloister came through Monica Furlong's biography of Thomas Merton, which I read while in graduate school. In describing the simplicity of life at Gethsemani Abbey in the 1940s, when Merton first entered the life, Furlong depicted a world of hard labor, austerity, and renunciation that seemed a galaxy away from my cushy air-conditioned suburban existence in a 1980s university. I felt in awe of the Trappists. It seemed to me that only someone truly holy, truly called by God, could embrace such an ascetic life.

After my life took a few twists and turns, I came to work at a monastery. I've already noted how meaningful it was for me to have this job and get to know many of the brothers in a day-to-day way. I soon discovered how down-to-earth (that is to say, humble) the monks were—most were genial and friendly, hardworking but easy to get along with. I enjoyed my fellow employees as well, most of whom were, like me, laypersons interested in the blessings and wisdom of Cistercian spirituality.

Still, no job is perfect, not even at a monastery. At one point I encountered one person in particular whom I found difficult to work with. (In all fairness, I'm sure he found *me* difficult to work with as well.) Looking back, it's obvious to me that the main problem was basic human nature—some people easily become friends, and others just never manage to get along. I wish I could graciously forge a good relationship with everyone I encounter, but that's certainly not possible. No one is perfect, least of all me! So there I was, working at a monastery, trying to relate to this one specific coworker with whom I just couldn't manage to connect.

I turned to one of the oldest monks in the community for advice. I confided how challenged I felt by having to deal with a work situation I found unpleasant. The older man listened carefully to what I had to say, and then, while neither defending my coworker or commiserating with me, smiled and said in a cheery voice, "You've got a saint-maker!"

"A what?" I asked, not sure what he meant.

"A saint-maker. It's a term we use in the cloister. You see, it's inevitable that when you enter a monastery, you're not going to automatically be friends with every member of the community. It's human nature. Some guys you really like, most you can get along with, but there always seems to be one or two who drive you nuts. Those brothers are your saint-makers because they are the ones that God uses to help you grow in holiness."

He paused to let me think about what he just said. "You mean that God wants me to become a better Christian by learning how to deal with this annoying person?"

"Yes, exactly," he said happily.

"Can I get a second opinion?" I asked grumpily.

"The thing to remember," my older friend said wisely, "is that *you* are probably someone else's saint-maker too. That thought is what really keeps us humble. We want everyone to like us but of course not everyone does."

The more I reflected on the idea of the saint-maker, the more I could see how it is full of gentle common sense. When I dislike another person, I seem to naturally focus on all the ways I want him to change. I think he should adapt his personality, amend his quirks, and erase his bad habits for no other reason than to make my life better. But if I see the person as a saint-maker rather than a *bête noire*, then I have to reckon with the fact that I can't change him but rather *I* may need to change. I might need to learn to be more accepting, more merciful, more forgiving, or more understanding. Or perhaps I should change some of *my* unpleasant quirks and bad habits. Obviously, when someone acts badly or hurtfully, such behavior should be challenged, but so often in life the things that annoy us about another person really do seem to be just matters of personality or taste. When I relate to others, even people I don't intuitively bond with, I always have a choice. I can choose to be kind and loving, forgiving and tender, or gentle and considerate—yes, even with those I do not innately seem to like. If we all could do this, then there is hope that we could all get along, and perhaps we can begin to live up to Jesus' mandate to love one another.

In case you're wondering, several years have passed since I learned about saint-makers—and I now consider that former coworker to be a good friend. So just because someone is your saint-maker (or you are theirs) doesn't mean things will always be that way. Nowadays I have a new saint-maker in my life—not a coworker but someone else with whom I struggle to be compassionate and caring. I've come to expect that God will keep blessing me with saint-makers for as long I shall live. After all, I'm not a saint yet, so I still have work to do.

"If you live alone, whose feet shall you wash?" asked Saint Basil the Great, one of the Doctors of the Church and an early champion of monasticism. This is an important question for all Christians to ponder. Not that there isn't a place for solitude in the spiritual life. Jesus encouraged his followers "when you pray, go to your inner room, close the door, and pray to your Father in secret" (Mt 6:6 NABRE). But such solitary prayer needs to be embedded in a life of compassionate and caring relationships.

In chapter 5 I suggested that hospitality is the bridge between humility and compassion. We can see the action of the Holy Spirit in our lives. First, we are called to self-knowledge, which involves the task of emptying ourselves of hubris to allow God's grace to heal and transform us. That inner emptiness makes it possible to welcome other people into our hearts, which is the essence of hospitality. Once we have invited others in, God calls us to form loving bonds with them—in other words, to form compassionate community.

The Cistercian way of life rests on the idea that spirituality needs community. After all, what is a monastery but a community of faith, where men or women live together to express their spirituality in a collective way? This idea is true for Lay Cistercians (and everyone else) as much as it is for monks and nuns. When Lay Cistercians from around the world gathered in Lourdes in 2014 to reflect on their spiritual journey, they issued a document called "The Lay Cistercian Spiritual Journey." It recognizes that the adventure of faith "is lived out in community with others," and goes on to speak of "the central place of community . . . as a means of spiritual growth." A community can be a source of "support and joy" but "also creates constraints, requiring patience, listening, and could cause suffering." For Lay Cistercians "community is an essential and indispensable element of our journey, a necessary means of spiritual growth."[1]

Nobody can single-handedly form their own ideal community. When novice monks or nuns join a monastery, they enter a community with the brothers or sisters who share the monastic life with them. Everyone has a part to play in forming and sustaining the bonds that unite them together. They work together, pray together, study together, and live together. Lay Cistercians, who build spiritual communities in relationship with a sponsoring monastery, create a bond with one another as well, but it is more spiritual in nature since it is a community of people who live in many different places, work at many different careers, and who probably see each other only one or two days a month. The monastic emphasis on community can be an inspiration for everyone, even those of us who don't live in a cloister. But laypeople need to be much more intentional about finding and supporting the communities in their lives. I do mean *communities* in the plural, for most of us have multiple associations in our lives. We all have family and friends, our workplaces, our neighborhoods, our churches or parishes, and other communities, formal or informal, that may be related to special interests, hobbies, or values.

It seems to be human nature that everyone needs both solitude and community, although different personality types may have to balance those needs in different ways. This paradox shows up in Jesus' teachings. He told his followers to pray in secret but also to love one another. The two great commandments have both a solitary and communal dimension: love God (in our own hearts as well as in the company of others) and love neighbors (obviously communal, yet to be healthy in our love, we require times of rest and solitude). Cistercian spirituality with its emphasis on silence certainly is conducive to solitude, and many are drawn to monasteries because they are places where times of solitude can be deeply refreshing. But Cistercian spirituality also emphasizes relationship and connectivity with others as a way to connect with God.

Many people tend to think of spirituality in individualistic or even private terms. It's about my personal relationship with God or Christ. Because of this, we don't always recognize the importance of community and may even see it as an obstacle to spirituality rather than as an essential aspect of loving God. Some even say "I'm spiritual but not religious," which seems to be a code for "My personal relationship with God matters to me, but I don't need or want a community to infringe upon that."

To appreciate Cistercian spirituality with its historical emphasis on community, maybe we need to try to understand the meaning of community better.

The renowned poet and Christian philosopher Wendell Berry's definition of *community* might be a useful starting point. "By community, I mean the commonwealth and common interests, commonly understood, of people living together in a place and wishing to continue to do so. . . . A community identifies itself by an understood mutuality of interests. But it lives and acts by the common virtues of trust, goodwill, forbearance, self-restraint, compassion, and forgiveness."[2]

In a similar way, Thomas Merton said that a Cistercian (and, by extension, all Christians) must be able "to live sociably, simply and charitably with others."[3] So a community is more than just a group of people who like the same things. It includes a commitment to be together, to stay together, to grow together, and to forgive one another given the inevitable bumps in the road that life will put in our path. To form community we must love one another.

But often we aren't very good at that. We barely manage to love our spouse and our children (and the divorce rate and incidence of child abuse shows that too many of us fail at this as well). We all want to be loved, to be enjoyed, supported, understood, and helped out in our times of need. However, community really only happens when we begin to practice compassion and kindness—when we begin to *give* love, forgiveness, mercy, understanding, support (material as well as spiritual), and help to others. Such compassion and kindness is crucial with people in our communities, although as Christians we also recognize the necessity of relating lovingly to *all* people.

The first generation of Cistercians described their way of life as a "school of charity." Not charity in the sense of "giving to the poor" but in the sense of compassionate love. One of the purposes of a monastery is to help human beings, broken and wounded by sin, to learn the ways of God's unconditional love for us because God is the source of all compassion and charity. And what's true of a monastery is true of any spiritual community. Community helps us to recognize God's love at work in the lives of others and to learn how to let that love flow among us so that we may truly begin to love our neighbors as ourselves. "God is love," bluntly states the New Testament, so if we mean it when we say we "seek God" then we are in fact seeking love, kindness, benevolence, forgiveness, mercy—for ourselves but also for others, even those we might not naturally like very much. Even our saint-makers. Even the people who offend our moral sensibilities. And if we take Jesus seriously, even our enemies.

According to Santiago Fidel Ordóñez, O.C.S.O., both Benedictine and Cistercian traditions regard community "as a school of love transforming the monk or nun into the image of Christ."[4] Here we are getting to the heart of the matter and not just for monastics, but for all of Christ's faithful. Any community that is centered in Christ can be used by the Holy Spirit, through love, to transform its members into the image of Christ—or, as the Bible says, the image and likeness of God, which is our original identity anyway. So it's less about *transformation* and more truly about *remembering* who we really are, in the grace of God and the love of Christ.

In traditional Catholic language, the Church, the worldwide community of faith, is called "the mystical Body of Christ." This has biblical roots, for Saint Paul described Christians as both the body of Christ (see 1 Corinthians 12:27) and also as possessing the mind of Christ (see 1 Corinthians 2:16). If this language seems too elevated or abstract for you, here's another way to approach it. We are called to *embody* the love of God in our lives. Not just talk about it or think about it or pray about it. We must live it in our guts, our muscles, our hearts, our eyes, our ears, and our tongues. We manifest that love when we share the ordinary rhythm of life with others who are likewise seeking to grow in love and compassion. Such love naturally expresses itself communally, even *within* God: Christians recognize in God a trinity of persons, traditionally called the Father, Son, and Holy Spirit; it is their self-giving love for one another which, in Dante's words, "moves the sun and other stars." Divine love is the source of all forms of genuine love, from the heroic charity of someone like Blessed Mother Teresa to the ordinary bonds that hold an average family together. God is love, and so it is divine love that enables ordinary people like you and me to get along with one another.

Divine love helps us to escape the shackles of narcissism or excessive individualism. Cistercian spirituality is a key that unlocks the chains, but we still have to make the effort to embrace our God-given freedom. We find love by giving ourselves joyfully to God and to one another. We love by choosing to repent when we make mistakes and to forgive when others' mistakes impact us. Giving ourselves to love means we joyfully receive the unconditional love of God as well as the broken-but-trying love of our fellow human beings. There is a mutuality to love, a sharing give-and-take that makes love dynamic, flowing, ever-evolving, and expansive.

To enroll in the school of love, to embrace the life lessons that come through community, means stepping outside our comfort zones, our self-drawn boxes of safety, and embracing the adventures that God has in store for us; where God is in control, love and mercy are the purpose and the healing of the entire world is the goal.

"Do not imprison within the narrow limits of your heart a generosity that is common to all," insists Gilbert of Hoyland, a twelfth-century Cistercian abbot.[5]

Likewise, in the prologue of the *Rule*, Saint Benedict describes the journey of spiritual growth as "our hearts overflowing with the inexpressible delight of love."[6] Traditionally speaking, love emerges from the heart—which is a symbol for the body as a whole, reminding us that love is not just a happy thought but a lived reality. We must learn how to love, and we must do so in a fully embodied way.

If you are like me, consciously aware of how often you fail at love, then this might seem an overwhelming task—to enroll in the school of charity, to give ourselves completely to the love of God so that we might be transformed into the image of Christ. Such a challenge is beyond us but not beyond God. As Jesus said, "What is impossible for mortals is possible for God" (Lk 18:27). This brings us back to both humility and the necessity of prayer, recurring themes of Cistercian spirituality. It also points ultimately to the type of prayer most specifically associated with the Cistercian Charism: contemplation, the "prayer of the heart." To truly manifest compassion, we must learn to receive it from the true source of all love: from God. It is for this love that we are called to pray, both with words and in silence.

It's ironic that in a world with more than seven billion human beings so many people are lonely and hunger for community. The Cistercian way of life reminds us that true community can only be found in God. I invite you to give yourself to God so that God may use you to share love with others—bringing hope into our lonely and wounded world.

QUESTIONS FOR REFLECTION

- Can you identify any saint-makers in your life, either past or present? What have you learned from such persons? In all honesty, do you know if you have ever been someone else's saint-maker?
- Can you name the various communities that shape your life: family, neighborhood, religious, work-related, or others? Are there any communities where you have a leadership role?

- Cistercians call their way of life a "school of love." How do you think God uses community to help us grow in love? Can you name some examples of this in your life?

SPIRITUAL PRACTICE: CONNECTING WITH A SOUL FRIEND

Community is a buzz-word that gets used a lot, especially in religious and spiritual circles, perhaps because our society seems geared much more toward individualism than toward the collective web of relationships to which God calls us. We build houses like fortresses in gated subdivisions where every family is expected to fend for itself, amass its own unique set of possessions, and basically mind its own business while all the other households do the same. Even in religious settings, where churches intentionally seek to create ties of fellowship, it seems that many connections are superficial at best. We worship together, serve on committees together, and if we really feel an affinity with someone we might occasionally invite them over for dinner. But that's about the extent of "community," at least for many people.

Against the isolating tendencies of our society, Cistercian life stands as a kind of counterculture. Monastics come from different families, different economic backgrounds, and different homelands. Yet in the cloister they are formed by bonds of charity into a lifelong committed community. Most monasteries also form meaningful relations with their neighbors, from providing a place for worship and retreat to charitable activities such as running a food bank. How can those of us who do not live in monasteries apply the monastic wisdom of community and compassion to our lives?

It might be best to do so "one person at a time." A true community consists of a web or network of relationships that we participate in organically. Finding or forming such a community can only happen slowly, over time. That's okay. What matters is a willingness to open our hearts to others (even just one "other") in order to create the space in our lives for the Holy Spirit to build real, loving relationships, which is the foundation on which communities form.

A logical first step for anyone seeking to be faithful to God's commandment to "love one another" is to seek at least one companion in faith. The Irish language has a beautiful word for someone who provides spiritual accompaniment to those who seek to grow in faith, holiness, and fidelity to Christ: *anamchara* or "soul friend." A soul friend is someone who encourages and supports you in prayer and your relationship with God. This can be an informal relationship, a prayer partner, or an existing friendship which deepens as the friends disclose their spiritual lives to one another. It can also be a formal affiliation with a person who has been formed in the art of spiritual guidance, offering direction to others in a more structured way.

Historically, a spiritual director was an older person who provided instruction and guidance to someone embarking on an intentional, disciplined prayer life; this kind of mentoring relationship was common in monasteries. But such a hierarchical association might not be suitable for all people. What is beautiful about an informal soul friend or spiritual companion is that such a relationship implies mutuality, where each person provides support and encouragement to the other.

With a soul friend, we can share both the joys and the challenges of spirituality. The relationship can drink deep of prayer, meditation, efforts to start or strengthen a daily spiritual practice, and discernment for how prayer integrates with all other aspects of life. Spiritual companions often will pray together and enjoy times of contemplative silence together.

If you already have a soul friend or spiritual companion (even if it's an informal bond), make nurturing this relationship a priority and keep it as an integral part of your overall spiritual discipline. If you don't have such a person with whom you can confide, talk to your priest or pastor or the guest master of a nearby monastery for a possible referral or consult with

Spiritual Directors International (sdiworld.org) to find a possible spiritual companion. Such a relationship should not be entered into lightly, so if you meet with a person about the possibility of spiritual accompaniment, take time to discern if this person is truly someone with whom you can confidently share your spiritual journey. In Christian terms, the point behind a spiritual companion is not to find a "master" or a "guru" but rather a friend who shares your commitment to follow the Holy Spirit, who is the true master of life in Christ.

CHAPTER 7

PRAYER AND LITURGY: THE RHYTHM OF THE DAY

Prayer gradually clears our inner vision, makes us
sensitive to what is false in ourselves, and—by the
experience of the love and mercy of Jesus—gives
us the courage to let go of the illusions we clutch to
hide our failings.

—Mother Agnes Day, O.C.S.O., *Light in the Shoe Shop*

Three months before the Allies invaded Normandy, the Cistercians came to Atlanta.

To arrive in the heart of the Deep South from their home near Louisville, Kentucky, they rode the midnight train to Georgia. They reached their destination on a spring morning in 1944, the feast day of Saint Benedict, 846 years to the day after the founding of the Abbey of Cîteaux. King Philip I ruled France in 1098, but when the monks came to Atlanta, the homeland of the Cistercians struggled under the yoke of Nazism. On this particular day, Allied aircraft were pounding the occupying Germans with bombs as General Eisenhower worked on the plans for the D-Day invasion that would take place just eleven weeks later. However, the only thing falling from the sky in the Peach State that day was rain.

Fortunately for the traveling Trappists, a group of Catholic priests from around the state (at that time, Catholics made up less than one percent of the population of Georgia) had gathered at the Atlanta train station to meet the brothers, and they quickly loaded their luggage into cars before setting off for the site of the new monastery, twenty-five miles away from downtown Atlanta.

Today the monastery sits in the midst of subdivisions where many residents commute each day into the big city, but in the 1940s, Atlanta seemed much farther away. What would eventually become State Route 212 was then a dirt road that wended through plantations and working farms. The abbot of Gethsemani had purchased the old Honey Creek Plantation and sent a man ahead of the monks to convert a barn on the property into a makeshift cloister. That "barnastery" would be the home of the monks for almost nine months, as they set up a sawmill, harvested Georgia pines, and quickly constructed the pine board monastery—a simple wood-frame building that would serve as their humble cloister for the seventeen years it would take to build a permanent home. This was all in the future, though, on that rainy day in 1944.

By early afternoon, the Georgia priests had driven through the mud to Honey Creek, dropped off the Cistercians, and left to return to their homes across the state. The monks, facing an austere existence with very little creature comforts, immediately got to work. They set up an altar and began their lives in their new home with prayer. As the sun set, they sang the psalms and canticles of Vespers (Evening Prayer), one of the seven liturgical offices (services) that mark the rhythm of the Divine Office. Like monks all around the world, the brothers of Conyers, Georgia, have been praying the liturgy ever since.

Nowadays, because of how close it is to metropolitan Atlanta, the Trappist monastery in Conyers has become a favorite destination for people seeking silence and serenity in the midst of their hectic lives. When I worked at the monastery, these visitors would often come into the gift shop and ask for information. If they arrived at the right time, my coworkers and I would always make a point of suggesting that they go to the Abbey Church, where the monks would chant the daily prayers of the Divine Office. I always was impressed by how first-time visitors, who knew very little about monastic life, lit up at the prospect of praying with the monks. Everyone, it seems, knows that monks and nuns pray, that they chant their prayers, and that this simple form of devotion is both timeless and deeply spiritual. You don't have to be particularly devout or even religious to find meaning and blessing in the gentle cadences of this ancient form of daily prayer.

Prayer, more than anything else, is the heart of monastic life. Artists paint, doctors heal, businessmen sell, and Cistercians pray. Everything else that monks or nuns do revolves around this central fact of their identity as people of faith. They read the Bible in order to pray. They practice humility to support their prayer. They live in community as a way to help each other pray. Perhaps of all the gifts of the Cistercian way, prayer—whether praying using words as is the subject of this chapter, or the prayer of deep silence (contemplation, the subject of chapter 8)—truly forms the heart of this particular path to God.

"Prayer makes you different in your inmost being," declared Gilbert of Hoyland. He went on to add, "and meditation changes you into a new self and renews you."[1] We pray not because God needs it; our prayer certainly does not change God or in any way make God happier. Rather, we pray because the act of worship, of praise, of seeking intimacy and love with God is something *we* need, something that changes *us* with the potential to make us happier and holier than we would otherwise be. Prayer is a gift from God that all Christians may benefit from and indeed ought to do. Monks and nuns are exemplary Christians who actually do make the effort to pray, not just daily but all throughout each day.

Another medieval Cistercian, Guerric of Igny, described prayer in its various forms as an "exercise of wisdom" that needs to be central to the spiritual life. Guerric identified five such exercises of wisdom: "the Divine Office, personal prayer, lectio divina, our daily labour or the practice of quietness."[2] If we accept the idea that work is a way to pray, then each of these exercises is a type of prayer. Lectio divina, which we explored in chapter 2, is a practical way to pray with the Bible; quietness (silence) is a doorway into contemplative prayer. As for daily labor, the Benedictine motto, *ora et labora*, recognizes that prayer resides at the heart of work. Clearly, Guerric felt the key to wisdom is prayer in its various forms.

But Guerric isn't describing some sort of medieval practice that no longer applies to life in the twenty-first century. Dom Augustine Roberts, the former abbot of Saint Joseph's Monastery in Spencer, Massachusetts, wrote in his autobiography about how important the various types of prayer were in the daily routine of Cistercian life. In addition to lectio divina, contemplative prayer, and the Divine Office, he also describes "a fourth form of prayer which is often overlooked but of great importance, namely continual prayer, at work and at such times as walking indoors or outdoors, during meals, or during classes and conferences."[3] This prayerful ideal is what the Carmelite mystic Brother Lawrence described as the "practice of the presence of God"—in other words, a point where every moment, every activity, is a type of prayer.

Dom Roberts tells of a conversation he had as a novice monk with his abbot, when the abbot asked him to sing more vigorously during prayers. The younger monk demurred, fearing that his singing would be a distraction. "But the gift of yourself is the heart and soul of the Liturgy!" replied the elder monk. This became profoundly insightful for Roberts. "I saw in a flash—and for the first time in my life—how heaven and earth are ruled by the law, the principle, of self-gift. That is what love is and that is what true reality is, divine trinitarian reality and human reality, which is really human only when it is in God's image and likeness."[4]

With prayer we express love of Christ, and it is also a *gift*, in a very mutual way; for prayer, like all spiritual blessings, is a gift from God. Yet when we pray, we give ourselves back to God. "Here I am, Lord." A crucial moment in the spiritual life comes when we recognize that our relationship with God is something bigger than we can manage or direct. We are not called to control God (as if that were possible) but rather to *give ourselves to God* in a spirit of trust and acceptance—in other words, to let God direct us, rather than the other way around. As the effort we make to connect with God through words, music, emotions, and silence, prayer is the means by which we make this essential self-donation.

Yet prayer is even more than this. It's more than just a project by which we cultivate a personal or private relationship with God. Christian prayer always has a communal or social dimension to it, even when we pray in solitude. This is part of the spiritual beauty of monasteries because they provide a setting for both private/individual prayer *and* communal/liturgical prayer. Prayer makes a difference in our lives, not just in terms of personal spiritual growth but also as a means by which we discover God's love and compassion expressed for the world.

Over the centuries, monks and nuns have always engaged in a ministry of praying for others—for people who specifically request their prayers and also for the world at large. This is a good example for all Christians to follow: to keep the heart and intention of our prayers oriented toward not just our own desires, needs, or aspirations but toward others as well. When we pray for our family, friends, neighbors, coworkers, our community and nation, as well as our adversaries, enemies, competitors and opponents, the space to slowly, gradually grow in compassion and love opens within us. Since we pray as an expression of love for God and through prayer actually seek to give ourselves to God, it only stands to reason that the Holy Spirit will use our efforts in prayer—to the extent that we allow it—to slowly transfigure us into beings of love.

Monks and nuns enjoy the support of a community that prays together multiple times every day, where everyone is expected to take part in the liturgy in a public way. Those of us who are not monastics lack that kind of structure in our prayer lives, and most of us are happy with the freedom to pray on our own schedule. But this means it is entirely up to us to make sure we follow through on regular prayer. We do not have an abbot or abbess who will check up on us if we start skipping prayers, so we have to be truly intentional about our decision to make prayer a priority.

The Divine Office is one of the most beautiful, meaningful, and powerful ways to incorporate monastic spirituality into your ordinary life. Just as monks pray five or more times every day, the liturgy offers a poetic and spiritually insightful structure of prayer that anyone (not just monastics) may incorporate into his or her daily routine. But the Divine Office is complex and can be confusing for beginners and difficult to learn, especially if you are praying it by yourself. For this reason, many people find it overwhelming and frustrating. Their attempts to get closer to God are lost in continually wondering, "Am I doing it right?"

When I first became a Lay Cistercian, I struggled with the liturgy. The commitment I was asked to make was modest enough: to pray at least one of the offices (services) each day. But I chafed against even that modest requirement. My life was too busy, too unstructured, too freeform, and too spontaneous for me to be bothered by something like daily prayers. Or so I rationalized it to myself. I muddled along, praying from time to time and justified to myself all the days that I didn't manage to pray.

Then, about two years into my formation as a Lay Cistercian, I became involved in an interfaith conference at a local church, and through the planning committee, I met members of all the major religions, including Jews, Buddhists, Hindus, and Muslims. I soon discovered that the Muslim gentleman on our committee was unwavering in his commitment to daily prayer. We struck up a friendship and one evening over dinner he explained how Islam included a commitment to pray five times a day. No questions asked; no room for debate. It was simply something one did, just as brushing your teeth or washing your face is a nonnegotiable part of everyday hygiene.

Humbled by my friend's commitment, I asked him to tell me his secret. He laughed and pointed out that Muslims have learned over the years that it's important for children to establish a daily prayer practice. "You need to start before your tenth birthday," he explained. "Otherwise, it's a difficult habit to establish."

I love to think that someday, ordinary lay Christians will be as committed to a regular practice of daily prayer as are my Muslim or monastic friends. I believe that in the early Church this kind of commitment to daily prayer was much more widespread and only fell out of favor after the rise of monasticism. This is when Christianity developed an unfortunate kind of "caste system," where the monks, nuns, and priests were expected to do all the praying and everyone else was just responsible for living a moral life, showing up at church on Sundays, and offering their tithes. When I was a boy, daily devotions usually just meant a brief prayer of thanksgiving before meals and an equally short set of bedtime prayers. I imagine my experience is not that unusual. But part of the gift of Cistercian spirituality becoming available to people outside the cloister is a challenge to pray, to seek intimacy with God every day—not in just a perfunctory way but as a meaningful part of each day.

While it is natural to gravitate toward the kind of prayer that one finds most meaningful or enjoyable, I would like to suggest that the monastic "diet"—formal prayer, scripture reading, spontaneous/personal vocal prayer, work-as-prayer, and contemplative (silent) prayer—needs all these elements to be balanced. We have to eat a combination of protein, fruits, grains, and vegetables with the right amount of fats and carbohydrates in order for our diet to be optimally healthy. The same goes for prayer.

Sometimes, especially when we are trying to pray alone, it can feel awkward or self-conscious, regardless of whether we are praying silently or out loud. Guerric of Igny offers a word of encouragement here. He notes that, even if we can't sense it or feel it, angels listen when we pray.[5] But it is also important for us to listen to our own words of prayer (whether they are spontaneous or prayers we recite from the Bible or the liturgy). When we listen alongside the angels, we allow prayer to function on two levels: we communicate to God and God also communicates to us. In this way, prayer continually deepens our connection to our Divine Lover, even if sometimes we don't feel the connection on a conscious level. The Spirit, after all, works in us and on us at a very deep level—so deep that often we may have no idea what's going on, but it's going on anyway. Thanks be to God.

When we pray, we are giving quality time to God. This is true regardless of the type of prayer, whether our prayer is as scripted as the Divine Office or the Rosary or consists of spontaneous from-the-heart prayers. Prayer helps us to become conscious in our connection with God. It helps us to become more aware of God's presence in every aspect of our lives, even when we are not formally praying. I invite you to begin, or deepen, your own commitment to prayer in the interest of drawing closer to God.

QUESTIONS FOR REFLECTION

- Do you have any prayers you say on a regular or daily basis? Examples could include the Rosary, grace before meals, bedtime prayers, or the Serenity Prayer. How does it feel to recite these "routine" prayers?
- If Jesus came back to the earth in human form and invited himself to your house the way he did to Zacchaeus, what would you talk about? What questions would you ask him?
- Dom Augustine Roberts suggests we turn all the activities of daily life into a type of prayer. What could help you be more aware of God's presence with you, even in the most mundane moments of your day?

SPIRITUAL PRACTICE: PRAYING THE PSALMS

The Bible enjoins us to "pray without ceasing"(1 Thes 5:17). Yet how can we cultivate the kind of devotion that monks or nuns take for granted? Certainly one way is to pick up a copy of the Divine Office, figure out the instructions for reciting the prayers, and just start doing it.

But the Divine Office is a significant commitment—sort of the spiritual equivalent of running a marathon. For many people, starting a daily prayer practice may require a gradual strategy, like starting an exercise regimen after too many years sitting on the couch. This is something I recently did. I joined my local fitness center for the first time in too many years, and two good friends, a doctor and a weightlifter, both gave me the same advice: Start slow. Don't push. Apparently one of the biggest obstacles for out-of-shape people who want to start working out is the tendency to do too much too soon and suffer an injury.

Thankfully, praying too much will not likely cause you to pull a muscle! But the wisdom of starting small applies to a spiritual "workout" just as much as it does to a physical one. For this reason, begin your prayer "exercise" rather modestly. When the time is right, the Holy Spirit will inspire you to grow toward a richer, deeper prayer practice. But no need to worry about that for now.

Here is a simple, yet effective, way to begin a practice of daily prayer. Every day for the next five months, pray one psalm a day.

That's it. Each individual psalm can easily be prayed in a single sitting. Psalm 119 is the longest psalm; it will take you about fifteen minutes, but almost all the others can easily be prayed in under five minutes.

Then, after you've been through all 150, pray them again; only this time, pray one in the morning and another in the evening. Don't worry if you don't "feel" the particular emotion that is expressed in any one particular psalm. Your prayer is meant to operate a level deeper than mere feeling. The point is to begin to foster a daily habit of prayer, to make sure that you give some time, even if only five minutes or so, to God as part of your ordinary rhythm of life.

Pay attention to the psalms. You will find that you like some better than others. Try not to judge the words, but simply notice their meaning and how you respond to them. When praying, try to avoid analyzing the psalms. Save that for a different time. (If you'd like to learn more *about* the psalms, a few good books to explore include C. S. Lewis's *Reflections on the Psalms*, N. T. Wright's *The Case for the Psalms*, and Patrick Reardon's *Christ in the Psalms*.)

Keep in mind that Jesus prayed the psalms. Jews and Christians of every generation have found inspiration, solace, hope, comfort, and challenge in this biblical prayer book. When you pray the psalms, you are truly partaking in a prayer tradition that spans the globe and the centuries.

After you've prayed the psalms through once or twice, it is very likely that you will feel drawn to pray more. If you want to continue to take baby steps toward a committed practice of daily prayer, try adding these prayers to your psalms:

- In the morning: the Canticle of Zechariah, Luke 1:68–79 ("the Benedictus")
- In the evening: the Canticle of Mary, Luke 1:46–55 ("the Magnificat")
- Before going to bed: the Canticle of Simeon, Luke 2:29–32 ("the Nunc Dimittis")

These canticles and prayers are traditionally prayed at the time of day indicated.

Eventually you may feel like you are ready to take on the full Liturgy of the Hours. Again, I suggest taking it in baby steps: at first you might only pray one of the seven offices, which are routinely prayed at different times of the day:

- Morning Prayer (at sunrise or soon thereafter)
- Mid-morning Prayer (around 10 a.m.)
- Midday Prayer (at lunchtime)
- Mid-afternoon Prayer (around 3 p.m.)
- Evening Prayer (before the evening meal)
- Compline (right before bed-time)
- Office of Readings (can be at any time of day; corresponds to the Vigil that Cistercian monks or nuns pray typically in the middle of the night)

The easiest to start with is Compline, which is short (it can often be prayed in less than ten minutes) and easy to memorize. Morning and Evening Prayer, along with the Office of Readings, are the longest sets of prayers, so they are logical next steps. What's important is to *enjoy* your prayer. As you pray, keep God's love in mind so that your prayers become your intimate time with God. If you turn your daily prayers into a dour duty sooner or later you will become bored or resentful or will stop.

Remember, we pray not to earn God's love, which is given to us unconditionally; we offer our daily prayers as a small token of gratitude for the love freely given.

Many resources are available to help people learn the Liturgy of the Hours. What I find especially helpful is a mobile app called Divine Office (divineoffice.org) that allows you to download all the prayers of each day in both text and audio formats. It's a great help to pray every day. Also, a monthly magazine called *Give Us This Day* (giveusthisday.org) provides a simplified form of daily Morning and Evening Prayer that is convenient and easy to use, especially for people just getting started on the adventure of praying every day.

CHAPTER 8

CONTEMPLATION: THE STAR OF THE SEA

Keep in mind that God's first language is silence.
—Thomas Keating, O.C.S.O., *Open Mind, Open Heart*

Dante's *The Divine Comedy* is one of the great treasures of world literature. Written in the early fourteenth century, this richly allegorical poem guides the reader through a medieval understanding of the afterlife, beginning with the fires of hell, then ascending through the cleansing "seven storey mountain" of purgatory, leading finally to the mystical wonders of the celestial paradise, culminating in the Beatific Vision of God. Not only is it a literary masterpiece and a fascinating glimpse into the medieval view of the cosmos, but *The Divine Comedy* also offers insight into the mystical spirituality of its age.

As Dante travels through the three realms of eternity, meaningful companions guide him along the way. He begins his journey in the inferno, following the pagan classical poet, Virgil. In Dante's worldview, Virgil would be a "lost soul," since he lived before the coming of Jesus Christ. At the summit of the mountain of purgatory, Beatrice, a woman whom Dante knew and loved but who died young, replaces Virgil and leads the poet into the lower regions of paradise.

Beatrice was Dante's muse, an ordinary Christian who died in a state of grace and entered into the splendor of heaven.

However, she does not take Dante all the way to the zenith of
the soul's celestial ascent to God. When they climb beyond the
ninth heaven and behold the white mystical rose in which all
of the lovers of God together form the "Bride of Christ," Dante
turns to speak to his guide, only to find that she has taken her
rightful place in the white rose. Replacing Beatrice for the final,
most sublime stage of this glorious journey, stood "an elder,
robed like all in glory. Around his countenance and eyes there
flowed the generosity of joy, his look a gentle father's, firm
and virtuous." This mysterious figure was Saint Bernard of
Clairvaux, the great Cistercian saint, theologian, Doctor of the
Church, and mystic.

Scholars believe that to Dante, Beatrice symbolized the
mind: human reason, intellectual ability, and philosophy to
comprehend—as far as is humanly possible—the mysteries of
God. No wonder that on Dante's tour of heaven Beatrice would
only be able to take him so far. When they reach the mystical
rose, the greatest achievements of human knowledge reach
their limit. To progress further, Dante needs a higher guide
than the mind. Saint Bernard takes Beatrice's place. As she represented knowledge, so the saint represented contemplation;
this is the gift of union with God, given by God through the
medium of love.

Why would Dante choose Saint Bernard to be his symbol
of contemplation? Why not one of the saints from the New
Testament, such as Saint Paul or Saint John? Or one of the early
Fathers of the Church, such as Saint Augustine or Saint Gregory
the Great? For that matter, why didn't Dante select a great saint
from his own homeland of Italy, such as Saint Thomas Aquinas
or Saint Francis of Assisi?

We may never know Dante's reasons for making Saint Bernard the best guide to heavenly contemplation, but it highlights
Bernard's reputation as a great Christian mystic. Perhaps Dante
admired Saint Bernard because of his devotion to the Blessed
Virgin Mary (a topic we will examine more closely later in this
chapter). Perhaps he admired Saint Bernard's keen insight into

the nature of divine love. Two of Bernard's greatest master-pieces are a short book called *On Loving God* and a collection of sermons on the Song of Songs, the Old Testament book that depicts God's love through a series of sensual, romantic poems. Or maybe Dante looked to Saint Bernard because he recognized that Cistercian spirituality, which Bernard exemplifies, is anchored in contemplation, the highest and most mystical form of prayer.

What was true in Saint Bernard's day remains true today. Contemplation is the apex of the Cistercian Charism, the supreme gift of the Cistercian spiritual path. The constitution of the Trappists stated it plainly, describing the Cistercian way as "wholly ordered to contemplation." "The contemplation of God in silence and detachment from all things," noted Thomas Merton, "is, for a Cistercian, the supreme apostolate." In his history of the Cistercian order, *The Waters of Siloe*, Merton suggested that Saint Bernard's book *On Grace and Free Will* "lays the foundations for a psychology of contemplation. . . . But all Saint Bernard's works do that. This [contemplation] was one of his predominant interests."[1]

Merton himself wrote several books on the spirituality of contemplation, with titles like *New Seeds of Contemplation*, *Contemplation in a World of Action*, *Contemplative Prayer*, and *The Inner Experience: Notes on Contemplation*. Many other Cistercian authors, ranging from William of Saint Thierry in the twelfth century to Michael Casey in our time, celebrate contemplation as an essential feature of Cistercian spirituality.

But what, exactly, *is* contemplation?

◆ ◆ ◆

The *Catechism of the Catholic Church* describes contemplation as "a form of wordless prayer in which mind and heart focus on God's greatness and goodness in affective, loving adoration; to look on Jesus and the mysteries of his life with faith and love."[2] Put more simply, it's a prayer of the heart, shaped by love rather than thoughts, by silence rather than words.

Because it is "wordless," contemplation is sometimes equated with mindfulness meditation or with eastern spiritual practices like zen. But it's a mistake to see contemplation as some sort of secular or foreign import into Christianity— contemplative prayer has been part of Christian spirituality since at least the third century. Saint Bernard would never have heard of mindfulness meditation and probably had little or no knowledge of eastern meditation either. It is a thoroughly Christian way of praying, but it is so similar to meditative disciplines found in other parts of the world that it can rightly be understood as a universal spiritual practice.

Contemplation is not about suppressing thoughts or ideas so much as simply choosing to be unattached to the normal "static" of everyday consciousness (what Buddhists call "the monkey mind" or Augustinian friar Martin Laird whimsically described as the "cocktail party" continually chattering away inside the brain).[3]

Because most kinds of prayer from the Rosary to the Liturgy to table grace to intercessory prayer involve words, it seems that we're always using language to seek connection with God. Choosing to let go of mental chatter in the interest of "affective, loving adoration" for God in silence can seem disorienting or even anxiety-producing at first. But the key to contemplation is gentleness and relaxation. We gently relax into the truth that God loves us and that God is always present so we do not need to try to impress God with our pious thoughts. Rather, we can seek to bask in the invisible light of divine love through the deep serenity of the silence that exists inside each of our hearts, deeper than our words or thoughts or imagination can reach.

Many Catholics and other Christians see Mary, the Mother of Jesus, as a model for contemplation. Mary is described as "pondering in her heart" her relationship with her son (see Luke 2:19, 51). To Saint Bernard of Clairvaux, she was an inspiration for the spiritual life in general and perhaps for contemplation in particular. "Contemplate in silence what no long-winded discourse could ever adequately explain," said Bernard, speaking specifically of Mary. He draws on an ancient epithet for Mary, "Star of the Sea," to describe her as a beacon of hope for those whose lives seem storm-tossed:

> O you, whoever you are, who feel that in the tidal wave of this world you are nearer to being tossed about among the squalls and gales than treading on dry land, if you do not want to founder in the tempest, do not avert your eyes from the brightness of this star. When the wind of temptation blows up within you, when you strike the rock of tribulation, gaze up at this star, call out to Mary. Whether you are being tossed about by the waves of pride or ambition or slander or jealousy, gaze up at this star, call out to Mary.[4]

Mary, the star, guides the Christian over the stormy seas of life, and this can be interpreted as the stormy seas of the *interior* life. Inside ourselves, we often ride the waves of distracting thoughts, passionate feelings, or chaotic impulses that can divert our attention from simply paying attention to God in watchful silence, which is the heart of contemplative prayer. When we become lost in the storms of inner distraction, Mary, the star of the sea, guides us to the peace of contemplation.

Cistercians have traditionally been devoted to Mary, honoring her singular role as the mother of Christ (a classical name for Mary is *Theotokos*, a Greek word meaning "Mother of God"). For Cistercians, Mary is not a passive symbol, a two-dimensional image of womanhood that emphasizes such traits as submission or docility. The Gospel story clearly states that Mary consented to her calling to be Jesus' mother. As a young woman suddenly pregnant in a traditional society where she could have been killed for alleged adultery, Mary showed courage and remained strong in her faith. Her role as the mother of contemplatives ought to be understood in this light.

Contemplative prayer, far more than just a passive "emptying of the mind," requires an active willingness to trust God, who is hidden in silence even as we navigate the storms of our minds and hearts in an effort to faithfully behold God in his mystery. Bernard's image of Mary as the Star of the Sea reminds us that in contemplation we are never alone, even when our hearts and minds seem to be hopelessly tossed about by inner turmoil. Mary is our guide in contemplation, not the object of our contemplation but a heavenly friend who seeks to lead us to her Son.

Contemplative prayer sounds simple (be still and know God—what could be difficult about that?) but in practice is surprisingly challenging. God often remains hidden within our interior silence, leaving us painfully conscious of the never-ending drama of our distracting thoughts and feelings, which often seems to mask our interior silence altogether. In other words, God seems shrouded in mystery.

But this mystery is neither a puzzle to be solved nor an occult secret to be whispered among the elect but a hidden presence which cannot be comprehended by human language or thought. "Our faith needs the experience of conversion and prayer so that it can produce a theology that respects mystery," noted Bernardo Olivera, former Abbot General of the Trappists, "knowing that all our knowledge, in the presence of the Mystery, is but an approximation, and all our speaking, mere babbling."[5]

Efforts to pray in silence often seem like trying to find God through a kaleidoscope: an ever-evolving, ever-changing pattern of thoughts, feelings, images, ideas, distractions, and passions. This is not necessarily a bad thing. Our creativity, our zest for life, our understanding of faith and the values that give life meaning all tumble together within our inner kaleidoscope. But jumbled together with these are the fears, angers, old wounds, jealousies, trivialities, lusts, addictions, and sins that keep us enmeshed in a kind of inner prison. We are created in God's image, but we are also wounded—in other words, every human being contains the capacity for profound love and goodness but also for sin, addiction, and alienation. We truly are chaotic—at least at the level of thoughts and feelings. But beyond the kaleidoscope of our inner tumult lies deep and profound silence, the silence where we can discern the holy presence (even if it remains hidden from our awareness). It is the silence where "the peace of God, which surpasses all understanding, will guard your hearts and your minds in Christ Jesus" (Phil 4:7).

As chaotic as our hearts and minds may appear, God's peace remains always stable. The Holy Spirit invites us to gently set aside our attachments to our interior drama so that we might rest in God's unchanging stability. This is the heart of contemplation. Just as silence encompasses both *external silence* (the absence of noise) and *internal silence* (the cultivation of inner rest and mental calm), likewise contemplation points to both an exterior stability ("being still" and knowing God) and an interior stability (resting in the silence that never changes, beneath the noisy dynamics of the "cocktail-party" mind). This inner, *spiritual* stability of God's ever-present, unchanging, merciful silence, remains always available to us between and beyond the turmoil of our thoughts and passions. (We'll take a closer look at stability, a core value of both Benedictine and Cistercian monasticism, in chapter 10.)

Guerric of Igny, comparing contemplative prayer to the light of God shining from within, wrote, "Go to him and you will be lit up, not so much bearers of lamps as lamps yourselves, shining within and without, lighting yourselves and your neighbours. We must not only shine in the sight of men by our deeds and words: we need to shine through prayer in the sight of the angels and before God in sincerity of heart. We light in the sight of the angels the lamp of pure devotion. . . . Our lamp that burns before God is our singleness of heart in pleasing him alone whose approval we have won."[6]

◆ ◆ ◆

Why is this type of silent, wordless, watchful, resting prayer so important? Why isn't just reciting the Divine Office or reading scripture in the meditative manner of lectio divina enough? Those language-based forms of prayer and devotion remain important parts of not only Cistercian but Christian spirituality, and no authentically Christian spiritual teacher will counsel you to dispense with language-based prayer, even when you are seeking the kind of prayer that arises only in deep silence. It's not "either-or" but "both-and"—and silent prayer functions alongside more verbal forms of praying to help form us as followers of Christ and seekers of Divine Love. Think of it this way: every conversation requires both speaking and listening, otherwise it is one-sided. The Divine Office and other verbal prayers invite us to speak to God, while contemplation gives us the space to listen.

Contemplative prayer fosters an inner spirit of acceptance and receptivity. It reminds us that we are not in the driver's seat when it comes to prayer (or indeed any aspect of spiritual living). When we pray in silence, we actually embody humility in our prayer. We make ourselves available to God but without presuming to tell God what we want to have happen or what we think should happen. Rather, we shut up and let God take the lead.

A renowned Cistercian writer on the topic of contemplation is the Trappist abbot Thomas Keating, one of the founders of Contemplative Outreach, an ecumenical ministry supporting spiritual growth through the use of the centering prayer method, which is based on the teachings of a medieval manuscript called *The Cloud of Unknowing*. Keating has written a number of books about centering prayer, silence, and the spiritual life. In *Open Mind, Open Heart: The Contemplative Dimension of the Gospel*, he suggested that contemplation leads to the restructuring of human consciousness: "The purpose of centering prayer is not to experience peace but to evacuate the unconscious obstacles to the permanent abiding state of union with God. Not contemplative *prayer* but the contemplative *state* is the purpose of our practice; not experiences, however exotic or reassuring, but the permanent and abiding awareness of God that comes through the mysterious restructuring of consciousness."[7]

Contemplative prayer is not an end in itself; it points beyond itself to the ultimate end of the spiritual life, an "end" that is with us all along only we don't recognize it: union with God. We practice silence to open our minds and hearts to God so that we may be available to allow God to transfigure us from the inside out, so that the qualities of acceptance, trust, and listening for divine love and guidance in our lives might become the abiding characteristic of our entire existence. "We know the glory of His voice in the joy of a silent heart," said Agnes Day.[8] Put another way, we cultivate a silent heart so that we may know God's glorious voice.

Contemplation challenges us not only as individuals but as a society because ours is a society that rewards assertive, take-charge, type A behavior, and we want to do spirituality in the same way. We want to be in the driver's seat. But that reduces God to a type of servant, who exists to give us special experiences of peace, joy, love, and so forth. Influenced as we are by the world of entertainment (Hollywood, popular music, television, etc.), we think that spirituality should also be a type of feel-good enterprise, and we lose sight of the fact that Jesus actually wants to make us *holy*. This means that, if we truly open our hearts to him, he will lead us to growth (even if it's painful) rather than amusement or pleasure.

Keating understood this. "I am convinced that it is a mistake to identify the *experience* of contemplative prayer with contemplative prayer itself, which transcends any impression of God's radiating or inflowing presence."[9] In other words, the goal of contemplation—to rest in God, whether felt or unfelt, in wordless silence—involves the totality of our being at a level deeper than mere conscious awareness. Often the grace of contemplation may be operating in our lives at a level where, as Thomas Merton bluntly put it, we "may know nothing about it."[10] As Keating noted, "What is the essence of contemplative prayer? The way of pure faith. Nothing else. You do not have to feel it, but you have to practice it."[11]

It may seem on the surface to be the simplest way to pray: take time every day to rest in silence, trusting God's presence and keeping faith in divine love, forgiveness, and healing. But in practice it is profoundly difficult, not least because the cocktail-party or monkey mind wants an experience, wants to be in control, and wants to fill up the space with pious thoughts or endless devotions.

Generations of monks, nuns, and other Christians have given their entire lives to the practice and interpretation of this kind of prayer. Ultimately, the best way to explore silent prayer is simply to do it and to share your impressions of this kind of prayer with a trusted spiritual friend or companion. But if you'd like to learn more about contemplation, particularly from a Cistercian perspective, look at *Toward God* by Michael Casey or *The Inner Experience* by Thomas Merton. For a more general overview of Christian contemplation, *Into the Silent Land* by Martin Laird is quite helpful.

We have now reached the summit of Saint Bernard's three steps to truth: beginning with humility (where we discover the truth about ourselves), moving through compassion (the lens through which we discover the truth about others), and finally resting in the silence of attentive, wordless prayer (where we open ourselves to God's truth) "in which we are lifted up to see what is out of sight." I invite you to pray in wordless silence every day, even if just for a short time, so that you may open your heart to the gift of God's presence, whether felt or unfelt.

QUESTIONS FOR REFLECTION

- What are some things you can do to find or create more silence in your life?
- Is it easier for you to be silent in the morning or the evening? What are some other times of the day that you find conducive to contemplative prayer?
- Why do you think Saint Bernard saw humility and compassion as prerequisites to contemplation? What can we learn from his steps of truth for our lives?

SPIRITUAL PRACTICE:
BEFRIENDING SILENCE
TO EMBODY LOVE

Contemplative prayer is both the easiest of spiritual practices and, paradoxically, the most difficult.

It is easy because there is, literally, nothing to it. It is the prayer of resting in the presence of God by intentionally remaining silent before God. It requires only a willingness to remain awake and alert while prayerfully resting in attentive silence.

In the spiritual practice section of the introduction, I invited you to listen to the whispers of your heart. In doing so, you began to practice a kind of unstructured or "natural" contemplation. Now, I'm inviting you to go deeper. Stretch the time you spend in silence, and enter it with a clear understanding that attending to silence is, in itself, a form of prayer. You are never alone in silence. The Holy Spirit is always present.

Various methods or practices related to contemplation exist, including centering prayer, Christian meditation, and the Jesus Prayer (prayer of the heart). Most teachers of contemplation encourage aspiring contemplatives to:

- find a restful body posture (ideally with the spine erect, fostering a dignity of the body as a way of bringing oneself respectfully into the presence of God);
- be aware of your breath (since the breath is the most intimate action of sustaining life that each of us takes, and traditionally the breath has been understood as a metaphor or symbol for the presence of the Spirit of God); and
- gently focus on a simple point of awareness—an icon, a candle, the Blessed Sacrament, or a word or Bible verse that can be gently and prayerfully repeated, often in synchronization with the breath, as a way to hold your attention so that your mind and feelings do not continually wander off into distractions. Yes, thoughts and imagination will wander off, but a point of awareness becomes a useful, practical

means for returning your attention to silence when such wanderings occur.

That's really all there is to it.

Some teachers of contemplation recommend remaining attentive to silent prayer for a set period of time, such as twenty minutes, once or twice a day (although I think that Revelation 8:1 can be interpreted as a good argument for thirty minutes of silent prayer). Remember, prayer has been around a lot longer than clocks, timers, or smartphone apps. So the important thing is simply to pray silently, without fussing over how much (or how little) time is given to the activity on any particular day.

Since that's all there is to it, why is it so difficult? To begin with, resting in silence almost always conjures up profound resistance at the level of thinking: *This is boring. Nothing is happening. I'm a failure—my mind keeps wandering.* Such resistance typically will sabotage our intention to pray silently on a regular basis: we too easily can find that we are "too busy" or too forgetful to contemplate many days, and if we are not diligent, any attempt to engage in regular, silent prayer may soon be forgotten.

So a practice of silent prayer requires commitment that is reaffirmed regularly. It also requires a willingness to start over and over again, after "forgetting" or abandoning the practice. Often, it needs the support of others, whether a spiritual companion, a contemplative prayer group that meets regularly, or a Lay Cistercian community or other group that is intentional about disciplined spirituality. If you find that keeping a regular practice of silent prayer seems to keep eluding you, consider finding one or more spiritual friends who will support you and whom you can support in return.

Regular retreats or even day visits to monasteries can also be a great support to contemplative practice, as well as engaging in contemplative-friendly activities like walks in the woods, meditative arts like Zentangle or mandala drawings, or even just a willingness to perform ordinary tasks like cooking or cleaning in a silent and attentive way.

Contemplative prayer does not replace other essential spiritual practices like lectio divina or the Divine Office. In fact, contemplation needs to be anchored in other Christian disciplines to maintain its character as a silent form of *prayer*— otherwise, a daily practice of intentional silence amounts to little more than mindfulness meditation (which is not a bad thing, but it lacks the spiritual meaning and purpose that contemplative prayer entails).

See if you can foster a daily practice of intentional, attentive silence given prayerfully to God. When you embrace silence, you may find that you more consciously recognize that God is present in your life, even if you don't "feel" or "experience" that presence.

Christian contemplatives embrace silence to embody love. Both the ability to enter into silence, and the capacity to receive and share God's love, comes to us through grace. It's not something we achieve: it's something we receive, and the benefits of this grace emerge over time, which is why a regular (ideally daily) commitment to silent prayer is so important.

"Be still and know that I am God," spoke the Lord in Psalm 46:10. Contemplation is a way to respond to this call. Try it today. Be still and know.

CHAPTER 9

CONVERSION OF LIFE: A PROMISE FOR ALL TIME

We are all on the path to holiness and for all of us it is a lifelong journey.

—Trisha Day, *Inside the School of Charity*

One of the most commonly misunderstood ideas about Trappist monks is that they take a vow of silence. There is actually is no such vow. It's a good thing, too, for some of the monks that I've met over the years are quite gregarious, and it's hard to imagine them willingly adopting a life devoid of verbal interaction. Visit most Cistercian monasteries and the monk who greets you at the guesthouse, welcome center, or in the gift shop will likely be affable, friendly, and conversational (although perhaps not loquacious).

During my years working at the Abbey, I noticed how some visitors seemed confused when the monks greeted them with a friendly "hello." I soon realized these were folks who, probably thanks to Hollywood, erroneously believed that a monk who talked was somehow breaking the rules.

Because contemplation is so central to Cistercian life, it's understandable how important silence has been in this particular spiritual path. When the Trappist reform took place in the seventeenth century, silence became almost synonymous with abbeys that followed the strict observance. Since Vatican

II, however, most monasteries have adopted a common-sense approach to silence. Trappist spirituality used to be much more penitential and austere than it is now, but even then no monk or nun ever took a *vow* of silence. Rather, they take vows that support their lifelong commitment to their community, their way of life, and their ongoing relationship with God. While the vows themselves are only appropriate for monastics, the meaning of the vows can be an inspiration to all.

Many people might primarily associate the idea of vows with marriage: "to have and to hold, from this day forward, for better, for worse . . ." A *vow* is a commitment, and in a religious sense, it's a binding commitment made before God and the entire faith community. Vows are serious matters, meant to last a lifetime. For monks and nuns, who accept a life of celibacy given to God, marriage vows are not part of their life journey, but instead they make vows related to the specific character of their religious order.

For example, Franciscan friars and nuns make vows of poverty, chastity, and obedience, known as the *evangelical vows*. Cistercians, by contrast, make vows according to *The Rule of Saint Benedict*. Benedict wrote, "When [a new monk] is to be received, he comes before the whole community in the oratory and promises stability, fidelity to monastic life, and obedience."

While these monastic vows are different from the evangelical vows, they cover much the same ground. Both sets of vows include obedience, and the Benedictine vow of fidelity to monastic life includes a commitment to living simply (in poverty) and chastely.

Those of us not called to become monks will never make a formal religious vow except for maybe our marriage vows. But just because we don't make a vow of such spiritual qualities as obedience or fidelity doesn't mean that we can't integrate them into our lives. In the meaning of the vows we can find insight, inspiration, and guidance for our journeys of faith outside the cloister. The vows can represent a challenge to us, to grow in how we give ourselves to the love of God. Such a challenge to grow is a gift for our ongoing spiritual journey, so the vows, like other elements of the Cistercian Charism, are "gifts"—even for those of us who will never make vows in this particular way. We may not make a *vow* of stability or fidelity, but such spiritual qualities may still be important parts of our own adventure with God.

The word *vow* comes from the Latin word *votum*, which means a spiritual promise, a solemn pledge, or a dedication. It also carries a sense of desire, longing, and prayer. Incidentally, it's the same word from which we get English words like *votive* (the candles we see flickering in old churches, each one representing a prayer) and even *vote* (a vote, after all, is a pledge of support for a candidate).

Vows involve making a commitment, being intentional, and making a choice. When we decide to walk a spiritual path, we are embracing a certain way of life, a specific set of values, or a particular worldview. For Christians, we choose to follow Jesus, to conform our lives to his teachings. This intentional commitment begins with Baptism, a sacrament by which we are initiated into membership in the mystical Body of Christ, the Church. Spiritually speaking, Baptism is more than just a happy ceremony: it marks us as belonging to Christ, forever. So the Christian spiritual journey begins with Baptism and continues for the rest of our lives. As followers of Christ, we choose to obey his commands, from the most commonsense ("don't worry about the future") to the most challenging ("love your enemies"). The Benedictine-Cistercian vows of stability, obedience, and fidelity to monastic life are meant to help a monk or nun fulfill the higher calling of following Christ.

So how does the meaning of these vows and the commitments they symbolize help us follow Christ? How can they support us in our quest for holiness or growth in grace as we seek to more fully respond to (and embody) the love of God?

We've already touched on the spirituality of obedience in chapter 3. Remember that the root meaning of obedience is "listening." For a monastic, a vow of obedience has a practical meaning since the ability to listen to others is an essential skill for anyone living in a communal setting (like a monastery). In a larger sense, obedience ultimately means listening to Christ and allowing his words to shape and direct our lives. And listening echoes in each of the three steps toward truth. Because a truly humble person is authentic, down-to-earth, and not self-obsessed, such a person often makes a good listener; part of true compassion and hospitality is the ability to listen well to others, and contemplation is, at its root, a prayer of listening for God in the silence.

Let's turn to the least well-known of the Benedictine vows: fidelity to monastic life. The Latin for this is *conversatio morum*, which can also be translated as "way of life" or "conversion of manners." The broadest of the vows, it's a way of saying, "I'm going to follow this way of life, and I'm going to let it convert me, to make me more Christ-like, to make my life and my character more consistent with the beauty and goodness of the love of God." Incidentally, this vow, for monastics, includes a commitment to poverty and chastity, since a lifelong vow of fidelity and conversion implies letting go of the desire for personal wealth or for marriage. For those of us who aren't monks or nuns, conversion of manners implies a more general commitment to living simply and being faithful to marriage vows or a chaste single life. But it means much more than merely saying no to greed, gluttony, or illicit sex. *Conversatio morum* means a lasting promise to let the grace and love of God slowly convert (transfigure) us into the very image of God. It entails far more than just "being a good person." This way of life is about letting God slowly remake us so that we can actually embody God's love, mercy, and forgiveness. A tall order. But the spiritual life is not something that can be mastered in a weekend—or a decade. It's a lifelong commitment. Each of the core elements of Cistercian spirituality (humility, compassion, prayer, contemplation) require a lifetime to learn. *Conversatio morum* acknowledges that we need time to fully accept God's gifts.

◆ ◆ ◆

When we embrace conversion of life, we are actually making a commitment to become holy—or, at least, to die trying.

Francis Kline, O.C.S.O., was the abbot of Mepkin Abbey in South Carolina before his untimely death from cancer in 2006 at age fifty-seven. Before his passing, he wrote several books about monastic and Cistercian spirituality, including *Four Ways of Holiness for the Universal Church: Drawn from the Monastic Tradition*. In this book written for anyone who seeks to follow Christ more closely, Dom Francis explores these dimensions of holiness:

- *conversion* (the gradual process of being made new in Christ by the grace of the Holy Spirit)
- *suffering* (accepting the Cross of Christ as it uniquely manifests in each of our lives)
- *desire* (longing and yearning for God above and before all other desires)
- *unity* (finding oneness in Christ and in all of God's creation)[1]

This beautiful understanding of holiness stands in contrast with the widespread misconception that sanctity has to do with escaping the world or denying our bodily nature. On the contrary, authentic Christian holiness begins right where we are, in our bodies, in creation, where we experience desire and suffering, and where we seek not a quick fix in Christ but rather a slow process of letting God's love and forgiveness draw us closer to him. All of this is so that we, in turn, may be a conduit of that mercy, forgiveness, and love for others.

Perhaps it has already occurred to you that the gift of fidelity and conversion is related to the gift of formation. God loves us enough that we are not required to be perfect or flawless (even though Jesus challenged us his followers to love perfectly in the Sermon on the Mount). And we are certainly not required to achieve holiness or perfection immediately. Because we remain imperfect, we more easily remain humble. Even so, God loves us, and we are always called to grow in grace.

This is one more example of how monastic spirituality gently undermines the idolatries of our immediate-gratification world. Our culture encourages us to assume that we can have anything we want, as soon as we want it, now if not sooner. But Christian formation is more like an olive tree than kudzu. It grows in a leisurely, unhurried way; it's built for sustainability rather than speed. In our desire to belong to Christ, we discover that his love is as immediate as it is unconditional, but our response to that love might only emerge slowly, gradually, over the length of many days if not years. When we make mistakes, as we surely will, we have not totally failed; we have merely identified the parts of our lives that are still very much under construction.

I don't mean to suggest that sanctity (another word for holiness) is a slipshod affair. An airplane mechanic's job requires complete excellence, for lives are at stake every day. Likewise, holiness has no room for sloppiness either, for our spiritual well-being (and ultimate happiness) depends on it. But it's not something we can achieve on our own efforts. Holiness is always a gift of grace. We try to make ourselves open, fully open, to God's leading. And inevitably, we stumble, hold something back, or resist the blessing of grace. But God does not give up on us. Always, we are called to continue walking on the path of conversion, to return to the place where we went off course, to press on in the way of life that says yes to divine love and no to narcissistic sinfulness.

In other words, conversion of manners—ongoing faithfulness to the Cistercian way of life—takes time and effort. It requires work and discipline. It is perhaps best summed up in the motto of Benedictine spirituality: *ora et labora*, which means "prayer and work."

"Work connects us both to Creation and to eternity" noted poet Wendell Berry, who also said, "If we think of ourselves as living souls, immortal creatures, living in the midst of a Creation that is mostly mysterious, and if we see that everything we make or do cannot help but have an everlasting significance for ourselves, for others, and for the world, then we understand why some religious teachers have understood work as a form of prayer."[2]

Saint Benedict, and indeed the entire Benedictine and Cistercian traditions, hold this understanding of work and prayer. Monks and nuns aim to live by the work of their hands, for they know that, at its best, work *is* prayer, and that work is (or at least can be) holy. This applies to "spiritual" work (overcoming personal faults, learning to forgive others, fostering a daily prayer discipline) but also to mundane labor such as earning a living, caring for one's property, or just doing the dishes. *All* work is potentially holy—not just the "spiritual" stuff. When I was a smart-alecky teenager, questioning my mother why I had to mow the lawn, she stood her ground and said, "Work builds character." This is another way of saying that we become people of virtue and character not by wishing it so but by making it through the unglamorous daily effort to do the simple things that need doing. What's true for human character is just as true for the spiritual quest for holiness. Yes, holiness is a gift from God but we prepare ourselves for the gift by striving to live a virtuous life.

So all aspects of life, spiritual and material, are subject to the conversion of manners. Everything belongs to God: our thoughts and feelings, the work of our hands, and the sweat of our brow. The commitment to ongoing conversion will impact the choices we make about the food we eat, the arts we enjoy, and our financial priorities. This is not to say that God calls us to a prim, puritanical life of pious perfectionism. Far from it! Remember, joy is a fruit of the Spirit (see Galatians 5:22), so a life of fidelity to God and on-going conversion is meant to be joyful, not morose. But it's a joy that is anchored in God, not fleeting pleasures or mindless amusements. It's a joy which understands that all aspects of life can be sanctified, made holy, when we seek this daily fidelity to the love of God. Even the most mundane elements of your day can be occasions of grace, blessings on the continuing process of becoming holy.

Henri Nouwen, the popular Christian author, spent seven months in a Cistercian monastery in the 1970s and kept a diary of his sojourn there. He reflected on the spirituality of work (and the work of spirituality): "Manual work indeed unmasks my illusions. It shows how I am constantly looking for interesting, exciting, distracting activities to keep my mind busy and away from the confrontation with my nakedness, powerlessness, mortality, and weakness. Dull work at least opens up my basic defenselessness and makes me more vulnerable. I hope and pray that this new vulnerability will not make me fearful or angry, but instead, open to the gifts of God's grace."[3]

I admire Nouwen's honesty. How tempting it is to reject dull or tedious work as mere boring obligations, far removed from the shimmering beauty of God's love. Yet when approached prayerfully, the most humdrum tasks might be the best means for seeing how God's grace extends to everything.

Conversatio morum calls us beyond just a willingness to be a hard worker. It's also a commitment to live with dignity and decorum. A friend of mine recalled how his father always reminded him that he came from a good family when he was a teenager (in other words: "Don't ruin our good name with your youthful hijinks!"). As Christians, we all come from the best of families: the family of the God of Love. So we are called to behave like a member of that family, with gentleness, thoughtfulness, compassion, and respect for others as well as ourselves. And if we keep our focus on trying to live up to the dignity that comes to us from God, then even our time for rest and recreation will have an elegance and beauty about it.

Thomas Keating wrote about two essential habits or dispositions that characterize the contemplative life: "dedication to God and service to others."[4] This is a restatement of Jesus' two great commandments: love God and love our neighbors as ourselves. For most of us, it takes a lifetime to get the hang of dedication and service. Thankfully, God is a patient God.

Conversion of manners is a spirituality of letting go, more so than always rushing after new concepts, ideas, things, or commitments. We don't need to go on a lot of pilgrimages, read a lot of books, or attend a lot of workshops in order to grow in holiness. In fact, most of the time the opposite strategy makes the most sense: we open our hearts to grace by surrendering the anxious tendency to always want to do more, more, more.

Cistercian spirituality is simple and ordinary. We express that simplicity and ordinariness by honoring who we are today rather than by always feverishly trying to improve ourselves. "But I'm so imperfect!" many might protest. That's true for all of us, and it's why I keep talking about spirituality in terms of growth. Think about it: a child grows without any conscious effort on his or her part. As much as our hunger for God translates into a desire to overcome sinfulness and self-centeredness, the Holy Spirit also asks us to humbly accept that even in our imperfections, God loves us and is willing to love others through us. And our growth in grace often may be happening below the threshold of our awareness.

Both the fidelity of *conversatio morum* and the deep listening of holy obedience lead us to one ultimate question: Are we willing to be conformed to the will of God? I don't mean this as a pious platitude but rather a complete remaking of our entire lives. Are we willing to say yes that radically, that wholeheartedly, to the call of divine love? Michael Casey posed this question in an essay called "Bernard's Biblical Mysticism." "Contemplation is a lofty state," noted Casey, who went on to say, "the beginning of this state of radical communion is to be found in our willingness to be conformed to the will of God."[5] In other words, the spiritual journey *begins* by saying yes to God, and this yes is not about how God makes me feel but rather my willingness to let God completely transfigure me into a new person, radiant with love. If my goal is, in Casey's words, a "high state of mystical union" (which sounds appealing), I must remember that it "begins with an ordinary level of zeal for the doing of God's will."

Casey went on to note that such "doing" of God's will is mostly about overcoming the selfishness and narcissism that most of us carry by virtue of being human, wounded by sin. So even if we have ambition to give ourselves as fully to God as possible, it starts in very ordinary, down-to-earth ways. This includes plain old hard work, a willingness to listen, and a commitment to the ordinary demands of a mature, virtuous life. We must learn to practice humility, compassion, self-discipline, forgiveness, and mercy, especially toward others but even toward ourselves.

Only monks and nuns are required to make a vow of all this. But just like the Trappists who don't take a vow of silence but nevertheless do seek to live a generally quiet life, we can follow their example. We may not be required by a vow to be obedient or faithful to our chosen way of life, but we can cultivate the spiritual virtues of patience, fidelity, and an ongoing quest to holiness just the same. It's all a part of a lifelong commitment to follow Christ.

QUESTIONS FOR REFLECTION

- A medieval mystic, John Ruusbroec, said, "You are as holy as you want to be." How holy do *you* want to be? What do you think holiness would look like, in your life?
- Can you think of reasons why God permits human beings to remain imperfect, even when they would like to live a more sanctified life? How can the Holy Spirit use our imperfections to God's glory?
- Unless we live in a monastery, we are not required to make vows of faithfulness or conversion of manners. But what can non-monastics do to make a serious commitment to God and to living a holy life?

SPIRITUAL PRACTICE: REVERENCE FOR WORK (TREATING TOOLS LIKE ALTAR VESSELS)

In chapter 3 we reflected on the spiritual practice of remembering the Sabbath. Giving ourselves (and our employees or land, if we have such responsibilities) time for rest is an important spiritual principle. But rest implies labor, just as day implies night or winter implies summer. We need time of rest because we are creatures who work and for whom work is good. Even if someone is unemployed or retired, he or she can still find meaning and purpose in work maintaining a home, volunteering at church or a nonprofit, or even the work of looking for a new job or preparing for a career change.

As Saint Benedict's motto *ora et labora* indicates, prayer and work are not opposites. Rather, we discover spiritual value through a prayerful approach to work. After all, *ora* (prayer) is a part of *labora* (work). When a monk or a nun performs their daily work duties, it is an opportunity to pray *through* the labor. Somebody once said that "work is love made visible." For followers of Saint Benedict or the Cistercian way, work is also prayer made visible.

One way to make this discovery comes from *The Rule of Saint Benedict*. Chapter 31 of the *Rule* offers instructions for the monastery's "cellarer," the person in charge of managing the community's tools and supplies. In describing how the cellarer should do his job, Benedict said, "He will regard all utensils and goods of the monastery as sacred vessels of the altar, aware that nothing is to be neglected."

In other words, even the lowliest and most unassuming of tools—shovels and hammers, hoes and brooms—should be handled in a spirit of reverence, just as a priest or deacon handles the chalice and paten used for the consecration of the Holy Eucharist. In this one simple sentence, Benedict undermined the human tendency to segregate the "spiritual" and "material" dimensions of life. How easy it can be to approach the spiritual side of life with respect and humility while treating the more mundane aspects of life with impatience or annoyance. For Saint Benedict, such a division needs to be healed by bringing that reverence and respect out of the "spiritual" or "religious" parts of life into every corner of our existence.

So let's reframe this with twenty-first-century tools or utensils in mind. How often do we treat our computers or automobiles with the kind of respect that a priest shows the chalice? Do we take a moment and consider that God is just as present in our workplace cubicle as in the adoration chapel at church? After all, God is omnipresent. It's just us human beings who so frequently forget to acknowledge the presence of divine love in the more mundane corners of our lives. But how would our lives be transformed if we *did* start acknowledging that presence?

This doesn't mean we must necessarily be reciting the Rosary all day long at work, reading the Bible during our lunch break, or other forms of overt piety. Cistercian spirituality is ordinary and obscure, after all. The point is not to be religiously ostentatious but simply to be mindful that God's presence extends into every aspect of our lives, even the bits where we labor, working hard to make money or keep our family fed.

See if you can come up with a way to remind yourself to be like the cellarer and treat the tools of your work—whatever your vocation may be—with the same kind of reverence and respect that you see the deacon handle the Communion vessels each week at Mass. Maybe a discreet reminder taped to your computer keyboard or on the dashboard of your car can help you to keep this idea in mind. It won't necessarily make a miserable job suddenly become rewarding or magically transform a difficult boss into a new friend. But it might have a meaningful (and observable) impact on your own attitude and feeling toward your work. This could not only make your work a more enjoyable part of your life but also extend your sense of God's presence in your life—*all* of your life—as well.

CHAPTER 10

STABILITY:
BLOOMING WHERE
WE'RE PLANTED

And like the fish, swimming in the vast sea and
resting in its deeps, and like the bird, boldly mount-
ing high in the sky, so the soul feels its spirit freely
moving through the vastness and the depth and the
unutterable richnesses of love.

—Beatrice of Nazareth,
"The Seven Manners of Holy Love"

A remarkable medieval Cistercian nun, Beatrice of Nazareth
lived a dynamic life, full of emotion and dramatic twists. But
along every stage of her journey, she learned lessons of wisdom
through her devotion to God. One of those lessons involved
the gift of stability. It took almost a lifetime to learn.

Beatrice was born around the beginning of the thirteenth
century. After her mother's death when she was only seven,
Beatrice spent a year with the Beguines—lay women who lived
in an informal religious community. From there she went to
live with nuns, who sent her to a neighboring convent to learn
the art of manuscript writing. At this time, she met Ida of Nivelles, only a year older but already renowned as a mystic. Soon
Beatrice received her own ecstatic vision, in which she saw

glimpses of paradise: choirs of angels, the heavenly Jerusalem, and even the Holy Trinity. Once the vision ended, Beatrice sobbed when she realized her ecstasy had passed, but also felt such immense gratitude that she laughed out loud.

Then she fell into a state her biographer called "the wound of sloth," leading to fatigue and inertia; Beatrice's normally devout religious observance became slack. Ida encouraged her friend to take Communion and to recommit herself to the routine demands of convent life. Still a teenager, Beatrice began to understand that spirituality was not about making requests of God; she also saw that extreme acts of self-denial could be harmful rather than sanctifying.

She immersed herself in the ordinary life of a nun, studying scripture, striving to grow in virtue, participating in the spiritual exercises of her community, such as the Divine Office and lectio divina. She struggled to cleanse herself of her sins but came to see that self-imposed penance did more harm than good. The young nun set high standards for her quest for holiness, continually giving thanks to God, and seeking through sheer force of her own will to be a more loving person. But she discovered that these willful actions could not achieve the sanctity she desired. Distraught, Beatrice prayed to God for help and, in response, realized that God wanted her to recognize something very humble, basic, and ordinary: God wanted her to see the innate beauty of her own soul.

She received a very simple, yet profound insight. God gives all people different kinds and qualities of natural virtues, each person unique in his or her gifts. Seeing that her soul contained its own beauty and that each person is a one-of-a-kind masterpiece of God, Beatrice felt free to follow her own God-given path of sanctity—which is to say, to become holy by being true to herself, to her own singular gifts and virtues.

Yet even this insight did not mark the culmination of Beatrice's journey. Eventually another long season of depression and inner turmoil returned. She feared that she might lose her vocation or succumb to sinful thoughts and temptations.

But during this "dark night" period, she also began to understand that even her spiritual struggles could be a gift, a way God could prepare her for greater holiness.

Despite the suffering of her apparent depression, occasionally Beatrice would enjoy a consoling vision or ecstasy. One time she heard God tell her that they would never be separated; another time she received a momentary vision of the Sacred Heart. But she also suffered physical torments in addition to her spiritual struggle, including fevers and physical pain (scholars speculate that she may have suffered from recurrent malaria in addition to possible bipolar disorder). By 1231, when Ida of Nivelles died, leaving Beatrice grief-stricken, she had developed her own reputation as a mystic and holy woman.

Eventually Beatrice was appointed the prioress of the Nazareth convent in Belgium, a community which subsequently became a Cistercian monastery. Little is known about this period of her life, but we can assume she settled in to living the ordinary, humble life of a Cistercian nun. Before her death at age sixty-eight she composed a brief mystical masterpiece, "The Seven Manners of Holy Love." This short essay explores how we are called to respond to God's love: with love. With poetic language, Beatrice spoke to how human love for God evolves over time.

The seven manners are:

- longing for God
- offering oneself to God
- suffering for God
- enjoying the splendor of God's love
- accepting that divine love includes both ecstasy and agony
- resting confidently in God's love
- contemplating the Divine Mystery of love (which paradoxically brings the seeker back to an ever-deeper longing)[1]

Beatrice beautifully charts a process by which we may respond to God through love. Of course, God *is* love, so the adoration we offer to God is merely a return of the love God has given to us. Lovers of God experience alternating stages of enjoying God's presence and suffering God's apparent absence. Enjoying the beauty of love while also suffering the inevitable pain of love comes with the journey. The highest stages of enjoyment, acceptance, and rest find love through contemplation, which bridges the gap between "earthly" and "heavenly" even while God's love continues to inspire a sense of longing in the soul.

So it comes around full circle. And even though Beatrice describes human love as undergoing many stages as it slowly grows toward God, the object of the longing, divine love, is itself unchanging and always available. In other words, it is a *stable* love. Because God's love is reliable and stable, it inspires the Cistercian and Benedictine emphasis on *stability* as a beautiful gift to help us grow in response to that love over time.

Beatrice came to see that everything she needed for spiritual living, for loving God, and for the slow process of becoming sanctified could be found inside her. It didn't matter which religious community she lived in or even if she were a nun or a laywoman. When she experienced suffering, illness, or depression, she did not interpret it (as we moderns often do) to mean that something was wrong with her surroundings. Rather she strove to remain faithful to her commitment to God and to her sisters. This faithful commitment marked Beatrice's stability, and in that, she found the freedom to truly discover God's love in her life. Growing in that insight pushed her to grow in God's embrace.[2]

Stability is the art of staying put. Human beings are not always very good at this, but God—who is eternal, changeless, and unconditionally loving—embodies stability. For monastics, stability is the object of a vow, but for all of us, it is a gift from God. And like all spiritual gifts, the gift of stability invites us beyond itself, back to the giver. Stability reminds us that to find God we do not need to be always on the move, always changing our life circumstances every time something doesn't seem to be working.

We live in a rootless society where we are encouraged to change jobs, careers, houses, cities, or, for that matter, marriages, political parties, and even religions whenever we are unhappy. After all, if we're feeling bad, surely something in our life needs fixing, right? So goes the reasoning of our world: let's not waste any time; let's make a change and try to make things work.

Now, granted, sometimes we do find ourselves in circumstances that are toxic or dysfunctional, and we need to respond to such external problems when they arise. Likewise, ambition can be a gift from God to inspire us to do and be our best. But how many marriages, families, careers, or bank accounts have been hurt, if not destroyed, by our collective, obsessive chase for "something better," something that always seems to elude the chaser no matter how many changes he or she might make? My gut tells me the answer is "far too many."

Monastic stability is built on the very simple idea that true happiness, true serenity, true contentment can only be found in God. Making a commitment to remain in a particular community, place, or circumstance is a way of placing our trust in God rather than in our all-too-human attempts to manage or "fix" our lives. For monastics, stability has a very real and practical application. By making this vow, monks and nuns commit to remain in the same monastery for life unless they are called to a new place for a worthy reason (to help establish a new monastery, for example). Those of us who live outside the cloister are not bound by such rules, and often we have very practical reasons to move to a new location or change jobs. How, then, can we incorporate the gift of stability into our lives? Since stability implies finding and sustaining our true *place*, I'd like to propose a two-pronged answer to this question. We can embrace this gift through the exterior stability of cultivating a healthy relationship with the "place" of our environment and the interior stability of finding our grounding in God.

Traditionally (from the earliest days of the order), Cistercian monks and nuns have been described as "lovers of the brothers (or sisters) and the place." Cistercian life is grounded in love. Naturally, monastics strive to love God first and also to love the other members of their communities. But they also seek to find joy and beauty in their physical environment: the place of their stability. It's a practical, down-to-earth love that supports the other loves (for God and neighbor). Jesus said, "Whoever loves me will keep my word, and my Father will love him, and we will come to him and make our dwelling with him." (Jn 14:23 NABRE). God wants to dwell with us. In other words, God seeks a "stability of place" in our lives and hearts. So especially for monks and nuns, finding a stable place to live is an external symbol of the internal *spiritual stability* that can only come from God.

One way the Cistercians expressed their love of place was in the names of the monasteries themselves. In his history of the Cistercian Order, *The Waters of Siloe*, Thomas Merton recites some of the poetic and bucolic names of Cistercian foundations.

> Cistercians were acutely alive to the spiritual and poetic possibilities of their surroundings, which they condensed into names like Fountains, Clairvaux ("Clear Valley," or "Valley of Light"), Trois Fontaines ("Three Fountains"), Vauluisant ("Shining Valley"), Aiguebelle (Aqua Bella, "Beautiful Water"), Senanque (Sana Aqua, "Clean Water"), Clairmarais ("Clear Marsh"), Bonaigue (Bona Aqua, "Good Water"), Fontfroide ("Cold-Spring"), Mellifont ("Fount of Honey")—not to mention other such names as La Benisson Dieu ("God's Blessing"), La Grace Dieu ("God's Grace"), Beaulieu, Bonlieu, Bonport, Cherlieu, Rosières, Clairfontaine, and hundreds more, all of them ingenuous yet full of meaning, bearing witness to a deep spiritual ideal.[3]

Stability means having a positive, mindful, meaningful relationship with our environment. However, it does not require that a place be perfect. *Cîteaux*, incidentally, is derived from the Latin word for "reed," suggesting that the desolate wilderness where the order began may have originally been a marsh or a swamp. So when the first Cistercians committed themselves to love their place, they were willing to do so even in the most humble of circumstances.

Stability means more than just staying put in one location. It implies simply getting to know and care for the place we live. Unfortunately, this is something many of us simply do not experience. Consider how rootless modern society has become, with much of our landscape paved over to make room for roads and our suburban subdivisions. Corporate office parks covered over with herbicides and pesticides to keep any hint of wildness at bay. Many people going days, if not months or years, without ever feeling grass on their bare feet.

Most of us have no idea where our food or water comes from or where our waste goes once we're done with it, aside from vague generalizations (food comes from the farm, water from the reservoir, and waste goes to the sewage treatment facility). Without disparaging the many wonders and conveniences of technology, medicine, and science, we seem to have created a world where many wander through life encased in a technological bubble. Thanks to smartphones and tablets, we have faces glued to screens, catching up on cute pictures of kittens or the gossip from people we went to elementary school with while ignoring the real, present world in which we live each day.

The gift of stability invites us to a different way of relating to the world at large. Without over-romanticizing a "back to the land" kind of escapism, the idea of being a "lover of the place" suggests that we bring spiritual values to how we relate to our home, our belongings, our region, and our environment. For some of us, stability could mean developing a more respectful relationship with the food we eat. Do we have a sense of the farmers, workers, drivers, and grocers whose labor made it possible for the food to reach our tables? Is our food grown locally, or is it flown in from someplace far away? What environmental issues surround the food we eat (for example, some species of tuna and salmon are endangered, yet are still consumed for food)? Are there political issues related to our food (does the farming economy where it is harvested depend on migrant laborers who are not paid a living wage)? How would our lives be different if we paid more attention to issues related to the food we eat and the people who provide it to us?

Water is another, related concern. Many parts of the world place stress on their water supplies as population grows and environmental toxins proliferate. Sometimes these issues erupt in "water wars" between states or municipalities. For an example from where I live, as metropolitan Atlanta's population grew in the 1980s and 1990s, the region's increasing demand for water began to create tension between Georgia and its neighboring states Alabama and Tennessee. Drought years typically make these kinds of situations far worse. Understanding the environmental (and political) issues surrounding water might be an important step toward having a more mindful relationship with this precious element, which could mean changing how we consume and conserve water.

But stability and love of place is not just about what we put into our mouths. So many issues affect the places where we live, work, and pray. How is the land in our county or state being managed? Is transportation infrastructure designed to meet growing needs? What strategies are in place for minimizing air and water pollution? What about recycling programs or other initiatives designed to slow the growth of landfills? Do our municipalities tend to dispose of waste in economically disadvantaged neighborhoods? What choices do we as individuals, as families, as neighborhoods, as communities, and as societies make today to ensure that the place where we live will continue to nurture families and communities far into the future?

As important as these kinds of stewardship issues are, being a "lover of the place" also implies, well, *love*. How do we enjoy the place where we live? When it's vacation time, do we immediately book a flight to an exotic location, or do we seek out a wonderful resort nearby, maybe just a short drive away? Do we support the arts community where we live? How often do we turn off the TV or the Internet and go enjoy a concert featuring a local musician who only has a regional following? How about a local artist or poet? When we eat out, do we always go to the restaurants that are national chains and can be found in every city? Or do we patronize local eateries unique to our neighborhood? Do we have an appreciation for the kinds of plants, trees, birds, and animals found only in our corner of the world? What rivers or other bodies of water are nearby? Do we spend time appreciating their unique beauty?

These are all questions related to the gift of stability that may be applied outside the cloister. Many monasteries are at the forefront of progressive land management or environmentally sustainable practices. So if we want to apply monastic wisdom to our lives we could do so merely by engaging with similar environmental concerns in our locality. To be lovers of the place means to apply this loving stance of environmental awareness and responsibility to *our* place—our home, our community, our bioregion.

I hope these questions are not leaving you feeling discouraged or overwhelmed. Remember the principle behind formation and lifelong conversion: we don't have to get everything "right" right away! The gift of stability is meant to inspire and encourage us to get to know our habitat, wherever it may be, so that as our knowledge, familiarity, and sense of connection with it grows, so our love for it may grow as well. That love is a sign of our *external* stability, which can support the *internal* stability of seeking to love God, not in some abstract, idealized way but in a real-world way that makes a difference in the here-and-now circumstances where we live.

To manifest the gift of stability in our lives, we begin by loving the place where we are, right now. If life circumstances lead us to a new home next year or ten years from now, then we ought to make the effort to love that new place. But for now, let's connect with the place right beneath our feet. Why? Because if that's where we are dwelling, then it is the place where we hope for God to make his dwelling with us.

Related to this idea of stability and loving the place is a recognition that happiness is not necessarily related to striving. Beatrice of Nazareth struggled with depression and health issues. Naturally, she sought healing but she also recognized that the key to her healing lay in accepting God's gifts *for her*, which may be unlike anyone else's gifts. Likewise, stability means finding joy in who we are as God's creations here and now (not just in who we hope to be, someday). This doesn't mean we shouldn't strive to grow in our lives, but such effort works best when it is grounded in love (love for God, for neighbors, and for ourselves). Stability in God contradicts the idea that we are somehow not good enough unless we make more money, get that bigger house, or drive the dream car. So much of the so-called rat race seems to be driven by this idea that if we don't keep up with our neighbors then we aren't good enough (whatever that means).

How would life be different if our striving was less about the demands of our consumer economy and more simply a reflection of our heart's desire for love, purpose, connectivity, and meaning? Those kinds of values seem hard to find when we live rootless, frenzied lives. They are the by-product of stability, if not in a physical place, then at least stability in a lifelong commitment to the love of God.

In chapter 2, we reflected on the sacred stories of our faith: the stories found in the Bible, the lives of the saints, and the writings of the Cistercian fathers and mothers. They provide a foundation for our life in the Spirit. As I bring this chapter to a close, I'd like to suggest that, for Cistercians, there are actually two kinds of foundations: one internal, the other external. The lore of the Bible and the saints provide us with that internal foundation, a foundation grounded in language, memory, and wisdom. But we also require the external foundation of the land where we live, the community in which we grow, and indeed the entire physical cosmos created by our loving God where we live out the days of our lives. This external foundation is what it means to be creatures with bodies, incarnate creations of a

God who himself became incarnate in Jesus Christ. Our faith is an embodied faith, and the Cistercian ideal of being lovers of the place and finding stability exactly where we are helps us to affirm the God-given goodness of this foundation.

QUESTIONS FOR REFLECTION

- On the surface, Beatrice of Nazareth's story seems filled with drama and inner restlessness. How do we find stability when our lives are full of turmoil?
- Can you think of a negative side to stability? What can we do to prevent it from becoming an obstacle?
- Identify one or two practical steps you can take to foster more stability in your life.

SPIRITUAL PRACTICE: FINDING FREEDOM WITHIN

Cistercian fathers such as Bernard of Clairvaux, William of Saint Thierry, and Aelred of Rievaulx practiced a form of meditative prayer known as *affective devotion*. It's a type of imaginative meditation, reflecting on the life and humanity of Jesus in order to foster ever-deeper love for him. This is an exercise not just to find peace of mind or greater awareness but to grow in love for God in Christ.[4]

It's an *inner* experience of love, and by cultivating in our own hearts and minds an appreciation for God's grace, Christ's sacrifice, and the beauty of the Holy Spirit, we can be inspired to respond to God's goodness through our own imperfect attempts to love. Affective devotion not only fosters an ever-deepening intimacy with God in Christ but also reminds us that, no matter what our external circumstances may be, we can find inner freedom through our efforts to respond to God's love. After all, God loves us the same whether we are living the life of our dreams or are struggling in painful circumstances. Embracing such inner freedom does not mean we avoid making truly necessary changes, but it can be an alternative to our society's pattern of living rootless lives where we keep making changes for change's sake.

Affective devotion is similar to the reflection step of lectio divina, *meditatio*. It's also similar to the Ignatian method of meditation as developed by Saint Ignatius of Loyola in the sixteenth century. Begin by reading a passage from one of the gospels about Jesus. In your mind's eye, visualize, as vividly as you can, this event in our Lord's life almost as if you were standing there. As you meditate, remind yourself that Jesus is one with God (see John 10:30) and that God is love. In your imagination, you are seeking a direct encounter with Love in human form. Try to reflect on the meaning and value of Jesus' expression of God's love. Look at how Christ not only showed this toward his disciples and the others he encountered in his earthly life but toward you as well. Consider how you can more fully embody Jesus' love in your life. How do you show it for yourself, as well as love for your neighbors and, yes, even your enemies?

Notice if your meditation actually inspires you to feel love for Christ, for God, or for yourself and other people. (If you don't feel anything that doesn't mean the meditation failed. Sometimes our spiritual work happens at a level deeper than our thoughts and feelings.) You may wish to reflect on your meditation by journaling or through prayer (which corresponds to the third step in the lectio divina process, prayerfully responding to meditation).

Affective devotion can help us, no matter where we are, to meet God in Christ through the Bible and through our own "inner theater" of prayer and meditation. Reflect on how this makes true stability possible, no matter where you live or how frequently you may have to move because of career or other considerations.

As we practice this kind of affective devotion, we may find that we are called to put the ideal of being a "lover of the place" into action. You do not have to be an environmental activist or an organic gardener to find stability, but you may discover that this down-to-earth spirituality inspires you to be more mindful of the money you spend, the trash you generate, or the energy you consume. Listen to your heart to see how you might be inspired to live out your stability as a follower of Christ. I invite you to truly be a lover of your place. You don't have to save the earth singlehandedly, but even the little things you feel called to do can make a difference.

CHAPTER 11

PERSEVERANCE: LIVING A (LAY) CISTERCIAN LIFE

The quiet mind of patience results from the action
of grace at a deep level that eludes our immediate
awareness.

—Michael Casey, O.C.S.O., *A Guide to Living in the Truth*

In the prologue to his holy *Rule*, Saint Benedict said that a monastery is meant to be a school for the service of God. It is a place to learn how to be a truly holy person: to walk the path of humility and compassion, to engage joyfully in a lifelong process of gradually obeying and conforming to the loving will of the Holy Spirit. Benedict describes this process with wonderful images, "as we progress in this way of life and in faith, we shall run on the path of God's commandments, our hearts overflowing with the inexpressible delight of love." The Latin words for heart overflowing, *dilatato corde*, can also be translated as "heart expanding" or "heart open wide." Saint Benedict saw that this school of God's service—what the Cistercians later re-christened a "school of charity" or school of love—would take us to a place where our hearts would expand, overflowing and open to receiving and sharing the delightful pleasures of the love of God, a wonder that cannot be put into words.

As I reflect on this, I am inspired to ponder the sheer miracle of the human heart. Kidney disease claimed the life of my daughter when she was still quite young. She passed away only a few months after her twenty-ninth birthday. Assuming she had a normal heart rate, by the time she died her heart would have beaten more than a *billion* times. For average human beings with normal health living a regular life span, over the course of our lives our hearts will beat somewhere between two and three billion times. Talk about expansive!

Your heart never takes a vacation, never goes on coffee break, never gets a sabbatical. It beats day and night. And every beat, every contraction of your heart muscles, is your body saying yes to life. With every beat, blood surges forth from the heart, bringing oxygen and nourishment throughout the body. The beating heart, in concert with breathing lungs and flowing blood, form a continual rhythm of life that blesses every moment of our days, from birth to death. And the heart is at the center of it all. Indeed, I would go so far as to say that every single beat of the heart is a prayer, an affirmation of life, a way of saying yes to life and to God, the giver of life.

After every heartbeat comes a moment of rest. The heart contracts, the blood issues forth, and then the muscle lets go. Just resting a moment, for then the cycle repeats itself. But in that split second, the heart is silent.

Someday, for you and me and all who live, the time will arrive when the heart beats one final time, and the silence that ensues will be the silence of eternity. For now, however, we encounter the silence of our hearts only within a succession of split seconds—beat, silence, beat, silence, beat, silence. Whether you are at rest and your heart is beating fifty times a minute, or exerting yourself and your pulse is racing well over one hundred, a tiny moment of silent rest exists between each beat. And this is the cycle of life: Effort, then rest. Work, then prayer. Words, then silence. Love, then letting go. *Labora*, then *ora*.

If every heartbeat is a prayer, then it is almost like the prayer of Martha of Bethany: a prayer that is expressed through activity. "Just as you did it to one of the least of these who are members of my family, you did it to me," said Jesus, reminding us that when we feed or clothe those in need or comfort those who are afflicted, we are doing his work (Mt 25:40). And while it's important to see this in terms of care for the poor or sick or homeless, it has a broader application. We do the work of Christ when we care for our loved ones and even when we appropriately care for ourselves. Every heartbeat is a prayer: it's the prayer of action, the prayer of Martha.

Then, when the heart rests, it offers the prayer of Martha's sister, Mary. When Martha was bustling about in the kitchen, caring for Jesus and his disciples, Mary sat at his feet, listening in contemplative silence to his life-giving word. The Gospel of Luke tells us that Martha was annoyed at her sister's seeming inactivity and complained about it to Jesus, but Jesus defended her. He stood up for silent Mary to distracted Martha. Many interpreters over the years have taken this to mean that Jesus prefers the contemplation of Mary to the activity of Martha.

But the Bible doesn't suggest this. If the tables were turned and Mary were complaining about Martha's activity, Jesus might have been just as quick to praise Martha's love, expressed through hospitality and hard work. Mary and Martha are sisters, and beneath their sibling squabble lay a deep, profound, and lasting love, not only for Jesus but for each other. Mary and Martha needed each other, just like our body needs both the continual effort of our beating heart and the rest that allows it to beat again. In our heart's rhythm of beating and rest lies a rich lesson for all of life. We need to say yes to life by making the effort to do the work we have been called to do. But we also need to balance our effort with times of rest, of prayer, and of contemplation.

The beauty of a beating heart is the beauty of perseverance. It doesn't let go, even as it continually balances its moments of effort with equal times of rest. When Saint Benedict invited his monks (and, by extension, all Christians) to embody the delight of God's love with an expanded heart, he was encouraging us to persevere in both *ora et labora*—prayer and work—with a steadfast heart to sustain our quest for the love of God over the span of our entire lives. Perseverance is like the vows of stability and conversion of manners woven together. Conversion is dynamic; it implies growth, change, transfiguration. Stability, however, is static, and it implies rootedness, grounding, and reliability. To find such constancy even in the change and growth that occurs over time, this is the heart of perseverance, and that's why it's the final gift of Cistercian spirituality we will explore in this book.

In the winter of 2006, the Trappistine nuns of Our Lady of the Mississippi Abbey in Dubuque, Iowa, welcomed five women who came to spend forty days living in the cloister alongside the sisters. These women were not interested in becoming nuns but wanted to explore whether the life of the sisters could have something to speak into their own lives. A reality-TV film crew chronicled the adventures of the sisters and their guests for a four-part documentary. (As it turned out, the series was never broadcast but is available on a DVD titled *The Monastery*.)[1]

The five women represented a diversity of backgrounds and values (most of them were not Catholic, and a few were even resistant to the very idea of faith). There were times during their stay in the cloister when they experienced conflict with the sisters or unhappiness at what they saw as an excessively restrictive way of life. But the women also found that the sisters provided genuine hospitality and that their simple way of life combining work and prayer provided a meaningful alternative to the fast-paced, hyper-competitive way of life that characterizes twenty-first-century America. At the end of the forty days, none of the women experienced a dramatic conversion. If they had claimed such a radical change of heart, the sisters themselves probably would have been very cautious about it, if not downright skeptical. But they all felt that their time in the monastery had been insightful and perhaps even made a difference in their lives. The sisters did not set out to win any arguments or prove a point about the contemplative life. They simply went about the daily rhythm of prayer and work and provided a listening ear when their guests needed to talk. That was all it took.

I'm tempted to say that this program celebrated the "magic" of monastic life, but that would be an inaccurate statement. It's not magic. The five women had to do their part, from getting up early in the morning to pray with the nuns to fulfilling their duties in the chores and work required to keep the monastery going. Because they persevered for the entire forty days of their stay, they were able to enjoy the blessings that sampling monastic life provided for them.

If forty days can make a difference in a person's life, how much more can six months, six years, or six decades make? The reason why perseverance is such an important value in monastic life is because—from the time of Saint Benedict down to today—monks and nuns have recognized that the blessings of their way of life are revealed slowly over the course of time.

If it feels like I'm repeating myself, that's because I am. We touched on this principle that Cistercian spirituality reveals its gifts over time, when we looked at the gifts of formation. Formation includes the understanding that God will take God's time in forming us (that is to say, restoring us) into his image and likeness. Fidelity is the promise we make to remain faithful to God through all the seasons to come. Perseverance is a sober reminder that spirituality is like marriage: God wants a relationship with each of us for "all the days of our lives."

This idea, that spiritual blessings come gradually, may seem opposed to the overarching values that drive our frenetic lives, where we continually look for the quick fix, the immediate solution, and the so-called power of now. It's important to live in the present moment, rather than to be lost in fantasies that distract us from what is real, here and now. But if "living in the present" means ignoring the wisdom of the past and denying the hope for or promise of blessings in the future, then it can be just as limiting as any life trapped by regret over what was or fear of what will come. The present may be all that we have, but it's not all that God has in store.

Faith in God empowers us to trust that as rich and beautiful as the present moment may be, even it cannot contain the fullness of God's blessings for us. In the incompleteness of the present moment we are invited to seek fullness of life not in our own selves but in the love given to us by God. Love—it is important to remember—does not yield its fullness immediately. "Love at first sight" sounds great in fairy tales and romance novels, but in real life it often can lead to a messy divorce or a bitter heartbreak. Even when love at first sight really does yield a lifetime of fidelity, the truest and deepest blessings of that love grow and unfold over time. So we find our fullest purpose and potential not in the now or in the imperfections of human love (beautiful though it may be) but only in God and in faith, which truly blossoms when we persevere in our love for God over time.

During his own extended stay at a Cistercian monastery, Henri Nouwen wrote in his diary that "a monastery is not built to solve problems but to praise the Lord in the midst of them."[2] After spending about half a year in the cloister, Nouwen, someone hardly naive about the spiritual life, was humbled when he realized that his life with the Trappists had not magically turned him into a saint. This is the other side of the experience of the women who visited Our Lady of the Mississippi; a brief encounter with monastic spirituality can change us, whereas six months (or even a lifetime) formed by the Cistercian Charism can nevertheless leave us struggling with the same old sins, flaws, and selfishness that we've always had to deal with in our lives.

That's the paradox of perseverance. We remain faithful to God, to prayer, to trying to make our lives better and holier because we hope to grow in grace and also because in some ways we'll always be a mess. I've told the story of a Trappist monk who says people don't become monastics because they're holy but precisely because they're *not* holy. They need the structure of monastic life to help them to be faithful to God. What is true for monks or nuns is true for everyone, for we are all imperfect. We all fall short of the unconditional love of God. If we yearn to follow Jesus Christ and if we want to love like God loves, then we may not be holy today but at least we hope to become holy. Or at least we wish to become more holy than we are. That means we want to continue to grow even if we are in our eighties or nineties. Our physical bodies may do most of their growing in the first twenty or thirty years of life, but spiritually speaking we can keep growing throughout a long lifespan. But such spiritual growth is the fruit of perseverance, the result of a lifelong commitment. The choices we make for today—to love God, to be faithful to God's call, and to make choices in the light of the Gospel—require a lifetime to blossom.

◆ ◆ ◆

"No one ever steps in the same river twice," declared Heraclitus. Change is a constant of life, and it extends to spirituality. Our relationship with God grows and evolves. "It is a bit of a truism that the reason why one enters a monastery is not always the reason why he stays," noted Cistercian author M. Basil Pennington.[3] Anyone who has enjoyed a happy marriage more than five or ten years knows that such a relationship necessarily evolves, if for no other reason than how the needs of life change over time. The passion of youth, the effort of rearing a family, and the gentle companionship of old age are distinct seasons of love. However, the commitment and fidelity that undergirds these styles of relating is always the same.

Presbyterian author Eugene Peterson wrote a book about the psalms called *A Long Obedience in the Same Direction*, a title which could almost be describing Cistercian spirituality. We "obey" (listen for God's call) in the "same direction" (over the course of the years of our life) even though circumstances, needs, blessings, and hopes will all change as that process unfolds.

We are always changing and, by God's grace, growing, but sometimes we experience shifts that may not be welcome (as in the decline of health that accompanies old age). Where is our stability in the mist of never-ending change and ongoing impermanence? In God, of course. We seek to be faithful to God through the vicissitudes of our always-fluctuating lives, knowing that God's eternal love is always lasting and always faithful to us. Sometimes it is easy to enjoy that love; other times we can barely hold on in the midst of life's storms. Perseverance means that we trust God's constancy more than our own chaos.

Confidence, trust, and patience are the keys to perseverance. *Confidence*, which literally means "with faith," is an act of the will. It means to keep relying on God even when it may not feel particularly fun or edifying to do so. We live in a world dominated by entertainment and seemingly besotted with the idea that only emotions matter. If you don't feel something, then it isn't real. Faith, the kind that enables us to persevere in our quest for God is, in our world, practically a seditious act.

But such subversion is holy in the best sense of the word: it orients us toward a life "set apart" for God (the Hebrew word for holiness literally means "set apart"). To have such faith is an act of trust. We count on God even when the surface circumstances of our lives seem out of control. Such trust provides a sane alternative to trying to manage everything on our own. We're still responsible for making the best choices we can in order to navigate the challenges each day brings us, but we try to make such choices in the light of not just our own perspective but that of eternity. This brings us to patience, the virtue of seeing the bigger picture and of recognizing that God's perspective remains so much greater than our own, which allows us to move forward with hope and even joy into the most fearful circumstances of our daily affairs.

The 2014 "Statement on the Formation of Lay Cistercians" stated that "an on-going conversion of life" is an essential element of spirituality.[4] That's based on the monastic vow of conversion of manners. Perseverance is what puts the "on-going" in "on-going conversion of life." Cistercian spirituality offers us practical forms of support to assist us in this quest for sustainable responsiveness to God. We need the nourishing words of the psalms and the rest of the Bible, the daily prayers of the Divine Office, the wisdom found in *The Rule of Saint Benedict*, and the teachings of the Cistercian saints to remind us who we are in Christ. We need to practice living the virtues like humility, hospitality, and stability to keep growing toward what God invites us to be in our lives. We need to embody the intimacy of silence and contemplative prayer, along with the relationships found in community, to keep us oriented toward the love Jesus asks of us: love of God, love of neighbors, love of self, and even love of our enemies.

Any spiritual quest has its tensions, and the Cistercian path is no exception. Such tensions include the emphasis on solitude juxtaposed to a commitment to community and hospitality. It's a yearning for stability alongside a call to conversion—the demand of virtue balanced with the imperfections of relationship, the ethereal wisdom of words and stories balanced by a celebration of the earth. What holds this all together is the identity given to us in Baptism, as children of the living God. For all spirituality, not just Christian or monastic spirituality, is ultimately about identity. Spirituality is not about what we do, it's about who we are. The "expanded heart" that Saint Benedict alludes to is a heart that has given itself to the love of God. It's an overflowing heart because God's love by nature gives itself away.

A loving heart is a generous heart. Most of us love imperfectly, so our identity as children of love, as generous givers of God's love to one another, will always be imperfect. But to persevere means seeking to grow in grace, in love, and our identity as children of God over time. And in doing so, we find joy. God is not just loving and compassionate, merciful and forgiving. God is happy. And to the extent that we strive to practice mercy, forgiveness, love, and compassion in our lives, we shall become happier as well. I am not promising you a shortcut to uninterrupted earthly bliss; but as we stumble our way, slowly over time, toward the light of Christ, step by step, little by little, we become who we are called to be, and it changes us (even though the job is always unfinished, at least on this side of eternity).

Over the course of this book you may have picked up on the paradox which is very much at the heart of not just Cistercian spirituality but Christian spirituality as a whole—the paradox which acknowledges that we human beings are sinful, wounded, and prone to make mistakes, and yet we are created in the image and likeness of God. The great saints and mystics say that sin—our capacity and tendency to hurt ourselves and each other by making unloving choices—has blurred the *likeness* of God in us even though we retain the *image* of God by God's grace.

"The goal of monastic life," noted Michael Casey, "is nothing less than the restoration in fallen human beings of the divine likeness."[5] This brings us to the heart of spiritual perseverance. We trust in God's love and mercy, knowing we are created in God's image. We are God's children, no matter how alienated from God we may temporarily be due to the foolishness of our own poor choices. We are always invited to return to the heart of love, and the slow process of doing so means a gradual restoration of the divine likeness within us.

Cistercian spirituality is a path for seeking God, but Michael Casey reminds us just where that quest ultimately leads us. "According to the teaching of many Church Fathers," he wrote, "particularly those of the East, Christian life consists not so much in being good as in becoming God. The Holy Spirit's work in us goes beyond the reformation of our morals. It is a matter of forming us so that we become sharers in the divine nature and, because of this, capable of fulfilling the impossible demands that the New Testament imposes upon us."[6] *Becoming God* and *sharers of the divine nature*—those bold words reveal the apex of Christian spirituality, traditionally called *divinization* or union with God. Such language should not be misunderstood as promoting pantheism or spiritual narcissism for the Christian mystery of union with God is grounded in love, not power.

As Casey pointed out, "Divinization is God's work and not the result of human striving."[7] Regaining the likeness of God, like every other aspect of Christian spirituality, is always and only a gift. Everyone is invited to receive this blessing according to the unique circumstances of each of our own lives. We are called to the heart of God's grace, to restore the beauty God intends for us, not to be proud or entertained or to have "cool experiences" but always in the service of love, to be a conduit of God's mercy for a world that so desperately needs it.

Such sharing in the divine nature might only emerge after years of faithful prayer, contemplation, and conversion of manners. It might take a lifetime or beyond; many saints and mystics insist that the fullness of God's likeness might only be restored in us once we surrender to the silence of eternity. Just as there is no limit to God's love, there is no limit to what blessings God may shower upon us in God's good time. All the more reason why lifelong perseverance is the final word in Cistercian spirituality and in any sustained response to God's grace.

How deeply and unconditionally God loves us! To truly and fully respond to that love will take the rest of your life, but that response can begin right here and right now. I invite you to embrace the journey.

QUESTIONS FOR REFLECTION

- Have you ever completed a long-term project (like building a house or writing a book) that required you to keep going even when you felt discouraged? What lessons did you learn, and how can they be applied to your spiritual life?
- What are the obstacles to perseverance? Two examples are discouragement and boredom; are there others? How do we overcome those obstacles?
- How does Michael Casey's bold statement—"Christian life consists not so much in being good as in becoming God"

—feel to you? Can you see a practical and faithful way to embody this "becoming God" in your life?

SPIRITUAL PRACTICE: CRAFTING YOUR OWN "RULE OF LIFE"

We have covered much ground in this admittedly introductory look at the beauty and splendor of Cistercian spirituality. Conversion, stability, prayer, liturgy, humility, compassion, contemplation, hospitality, perseverance are all core elements of the Cistercian way, but even when we hold all these gifts together we have hardly begun to explore the fullness of this rich path of response to the love of God. Perseverance matters because to truly grow in the riches of God's love generally takes time (even though God's love is unconditional and always present to us, always available here in the present moment).

One of the reasons why *The Rule of Saint Benedict* has had such long staying power throughout Christian history is because it provides monks and nuns with a *rule of life*. A rule of life represents a kind of a mission statement or declaration of spiritual intent. Such a rule can provide meaningful and lasting support to those who agree to abide by its demands. By "putting it in writing," we declare to God, to ourselves, and to others our intention to follow the contemplative life in a sustainable and lifelong way.

The Rule of Saint Benedict is designed for an entire community to follow. But many spiritual seekers work on developing a *personal* rule of life, usually in consultation with a spiritual director or companion, to provide structure and support to his or her individual responses to the Holy Spirit. Such a rule need not be elaborate or complex; it is a covenant, not a contract. It is meant to be a source of inspiration, or perhaps of challenge, and a reminder to keep growing in response to God's grace.

Your rule might include a description of your daily prayer practice: such as praying all or part of the Divine Office, practicing lectio divina, and sitting in silent contemplation. It can also include other life goals (for example dieting, exercise, paying off debt, or reducing one's possessions). It might be linked to your external religious observance (a commitment to attend daily Mass or to give a certain number of hours each month to ministries that support those in need). A personal rule of life, because it is personal, is unique to each individual and works best when it is crafted in response to your specific circumstances and sense of God's call.

A personal rule of life is not meant to be a guilt-trip. The reality of setting up such a personal statement of spiritual intention is that even the most dedicated person will sooner or later fail to keep their rule, or at least fail to keep it perfectly. That, however, need not discourage you. The best rule of life will challenge you to grow, and if you don't always live up to the challenge, if nothing else you get practice in the art of humility!

Since a personal rule is so individual, it can reasonably be revised and rewritten as needed. Some people make a point of revisiting their personal rule on an annual basis, typically in conversation with a spiritual companion. For others, every two, three, or five years might be the right amount of time to revise their rule. What's important is to remember that a personal rule is not written in stone and can (and perhaps should) be adapted in response to changing life circumstances.

If you are interested in crafting your personal rule of life, discuss the idea with your spiritual friend, director, or companion. Together you can discern how you sense God calling you to grow in response to God's love. Try to put that sense of calling into writing. Your rule can emerge from there. Here are a few questions you can ask yourself, to start the process. Think about these questions, pray about them, and then write your answers down as a first draft for your rule.

1. What do you currently do to nurture your spiritual life?
2. What daily commitments are you willing to make to foster your relationship with God?

3. What virtues or good habits do you feel called to cultivate in your life? What ideas do you have for steps you can take to grow these virtues?
4. How are you expressing love for your neighbor— especially for those who are in need?
5. What can you do to take care of yourself beyond religious or spiritual commitments (for example, what is your exercise routine, or how do you ensure you get enough rest and recreation)?

These questions are just a start. To explore this topic further, read a book on crafting a rule of life, such as Margaret Guenther's *At Home in the World*, Debra Farrington's *Living Faith Day by Day*, or Stephen Macchia's *Crafting a Rule of Life*.

A FINAL WORD

Monasteries are special, holy places. That's true of most monasteries, not just Cistercian abbeys, but since my topic is Cistercian spirituality, I am focusing on their unique gifts. We don't have to have a vocation to be a monk or a nun to appreciate the blessings of the monastic world. We might be drawn to monasteries because we love the prayer, the chanting, the rituals of the liturgy, the art and architecture, the landscaping, or above all, the silence. After we've visited a particular abbey a few times, we may find that we begin to get to know some of the members of the community, which just enriches the experience even more. It's like making friends in a foreign country. We know that we'll never be natives of the land, but by virtue of our friendships, when we go visit we are more than just tourists.

And that's really the point behind this book. I'm inviting you to be more than just a tourist when you visit a monastery or reflect on the spirituality of the monks or nuns. Cistercian spirituality may be the hidden jewel of the church, but thanks to the openness of Vatican II, the Lay Cistercian movement, and the writings of authors like Thomas Merton it is available to more people than ever.

Most of the elements of monastic spirituality are adaptable to the lives of people who live "in the world." Whether we are single or married, working or retired, childless or part of a large family, we can be blessed by the gifts of humility, stability, compassion, conversion, prayer, silence, and contemplation. These are universal spiritual values, and we owe a debt of gratitude to monasteries for doing such a good job at keeping these blessings part of their identity when our society at large often has forgotten about these spiritual treasures.

I believe that the ultimate reason people are drawn to monasteries (even agnostics or atheists or people who haven't been to a church in years) is because there is something deep in our souls that hungers for God. God is a mystery, and even the greatest philosophies and theologies ultimately fail to capture the fullness of divine love and splendor. But a monastery, in its ordinary, down-to-earth humility, can convey a sense of that mystery for ordinary people. We go to the monastery because we want more God in our lives.

In writing this book, one of my goals has been to encourage ordinary people (like myself) to be just a bit more mindful or intentional about that God-hunger. Notice it, be aware of it, and nurture it. That hunger is itself a gift from God, maybe the most precious gift we all have. For I believe that longing will eventually lead us back to God, if only we allow it. And the beauty of Cistercian spirituality is that it can be a helpful map or guide along the way.

Many blessings to you on your journey. May you persevere with gladness and joy.

ACKNOWLEDGMENTS

Many people have supported this book in large and small ways. I cannot list everyone, so let me begin with a general word of thanks to all the friends, students, colleagues, fellow Lay Cistercians, and, especially, monastics who have walked with me as I have written this book. I am grateful for you all. If there is any wisdom to be found in these pages, it is due to the grace of God and the wonderful support of those who have helped me along the way. Of course, any errors or blemishes in the book are completely my responsibility.

Lil Copan and Linda Roghaar paved the way to finding *Befriending Silence* a wonderful home at Ave Maria Press. Thanks also to Tom Grady, Bob Hamma, Jonathan Ryan, Katherine Rowley, Stephanie A. Sibal, Janice Rajski, and everyone else at Ave for your good work in support of this book.

A special word of gratitude to Brother Cassian Russell, O.C.S.O., who not only offered advice to help me understand Cistercian spirituality from a global perspective but who also arranged for me to receive permission to use the library at the Monastery of the Holy Spirit for much of my research—a rare privilege and a deep honor. To be able to write portions of this book in a monastic scriptorium was deeply moving for me, and I am profoundly grateful. Father Anthony Delisi, O.C.S.O., will probably be embarrassed when I say this, but I feel truly blessed by the privilege of knowing him as a mentor, a teacher, a friend, and an occasional deflator of my ego (merely to safeguard my humility of course). His witness as a Trappist monk eager to share the Cistercian Charism with laypersons not only made this book possible but continues to inspire me. Numerous other monks of Conyers and other monasteries, including Abbot Francis Michael Stiteler, O.C.S.O.; Brother Elias Marechal, O.C.S.O.; Father Tom Francis Smith, O.C.S.O.; Father Methodius Telnack, O.C.S.O.; Brother Callistus Crichlow, O.C.S.O.; Father Michael Casey, O.C.S.O.; and Dom Armand Veillieux, O.C.S.O., have been gracious and helpful as well.

Among the Lay Cistercians, particular thanks goes out to Francisco and Maria Ambrosetti, Phil Foster, Teresa McMahon, Linda Mitchell, Frank Mulcahy, Julie Magri, Jacqueline Rychlicki, Natalia Shulgina, Peter Alan Stuart, Rocky Thomas, Michael Thompson, and Patricia Tyson.

Others to thank, for various reasons, include Julie Hliboki; Mark Dannenfelser; Haven Sweet; Steve Yander; the staff of the John Bulow Campbell Library at Columbia Theological Seminary, especially Mary Martha Riviere; and my beloved community of Atlanta Shalem graduates, including CeCe Balboni, Lerita Coleman, Stuart Higginbotham, Barb Meinert, Joan Murray, and David Rensberger.

Finally, as always, words can only hint at my boundless appreciation for the love of my life, Fran V. McColman, and our daughter, Rhiannon. Shortly after I began writing this book, Rhiannon, who lived with life-threatening polycistic kidney disease from birth, made the difficult but trusting decision to enter in-home hospice. She lived with her mother and me until her death, at age twenty-nine, on August 30, 2014. As painful as Rhiannon's passing has been for me and Fran, the witness of the Cistercian Charism, with its deep faith in God, longing for heaven, and serenity in dying, gave us the strength to walk with Rhiannon in the final weeks of her life with peace and even a measure of joy. Fran's love for her daughter (and me), her self-giving care for Rhiannon, and her dignity in the excruciating experience of losing her only child, witnesses to me daily of the "love that moves the sun and other stars." Thank you, thank you, thank you.

APPENDIX 1

VOCATIONS TO CISTERCIAN MONASTIC LIFE

Cistercian spirituality can bless everyone. With this principle in mind, I have written this book for everyone whether married or single, Catholic or non-Catholic, even Christian or non-Christian (although, obviously this is a book about the Christian life). Wherever you are on life's journey, I believe that the wisdom and the unique gifts of the Cistercian path can be a blessing for you.

However, there would be no such thing as "Cistercian spirituality" if it were not for the thousands of dedicated men and women who, generation after generation, have given their lives to God by entering into and persevering in monastic life. Cistercian monks and nuns embrace the fullness of this beautiful, austere, deeply contemplative way of life, not only for their own salvation but also as a witness and blessing to others. Most obviously, monks and nuns give themselves to their specific monastic communities—to their fellow brothers and sisters with whom they live, work, and pray—at one of the many Cistercian abbeys found throughout the world. But in a very real way, nuns and monks give themselves to the entire Church, the mystical Body of Christ, and perhaps even to all people of all faiths, since monastics daily pray for the world.

Living their hidden lives within the cloister, given over to simplicity and continual prayer, Cistercians (like other monks and nuns) are a witness to a way of life that places love before profits, people before things, and God before self-gratification. By providing such a witness, monastics give humanity a precious gift. But they go even further. Since most monasteries provide hospitality to guests, and many also provide instruction in spirituality to those who become their lay associates, nuns and monks are literally helping change the world by providing instruction, guidance, and encouragement to countless non-monastics who seek to live in a more contemplative way of life.

So for those of us who are *not* called to be nuns and monks, we owe a tremendous debt of gratitude to the people who do enter into monastic life. Their lives, their prayer, their witness, and their hospitality are blessings for us all.

Now, it occurs to me that some people who read this book may actually be in a position where they might sense a "tug" or call to explore monastic life further for themselves. If you are Catholic, single, in good physical and psychological health, with no financial burdens or other obligations, *and* you sense a possible interest in the monastic way of life, perhaps this interest needs to be explored more fully.

Monastic communities rejoice when postulants enter into the life, but everyone's call is unique so not everyone is meant to be a monk or a nun. Anyone who feels a sense of attraction to this way of life needs to undergo a discernment process in partnership with the vocation director at an abbey. The process (and specific requirements, such as age limits) vary from community to community.

But in general, you can expect that a vocations director will want to get to know you over time, perhaps by inviting you to make one or more retreats and then spending some time in the cloister as an "observer." This is a time to allow you to become more familiar with monastic life and to meet the members of the community so you can get to know them (and they, you). After your observership, you'll be asked to leave for at least a month or so, to give you additional time for discernment. You will be expected to complete a physical and a psychological examination. If at the end of this process you and the vocation director both feel good about you moving forward, you may be invited to live in the community as a postulant. You will begin a period of study, prayer, and continued discernment, as you live the monastic life and begin the lifelong process of giving yourself to Christ in this particular way.

Would-be monks or nuns have a number of years to discern if this life is meant for them. After postulancy, which can last six months or more, the potential monastic becomes a novice. The novitiate may last for two or more years. Upon completing this stage, the novice can make temporary vows, usually for a one-year period. These vows can be repeated almost indefinitely, and most communities will require the junior monk or nun to make temporary vows for at least three years before going on to the final step of solemn or lifetime profession, when the vows are made for life.

Not everyone who is accepted as a postulant will eventually make a solemn profession, and that's okay. That's the point behind this lengthy process of discernment. But even those who eventually leave the cloister often report that this period of exploration proved to be a rich and meaningful chapter of their lives. Others, of course, persevere, and carry on this centuries-old tradition of prayer and contemplation, remaining in the monastery until they die.

Think this could be for you? Interested in at least considering the idea? If so, turn to appendix 3, consult the list of Cistercian monasteries in North America, and contact the one nearest you for more information. May you enjoy abundant blessings as you explore what God's will might be for your life.

VOCATIONS TO THE LAY CISTERCIAN FAMILY

As I mentioned at the beginning of chapter 5, the Lay Cistercian movement is relatively young, having emerged in the years following Vatican II. But from its humble beginnings with laypersons seeking spiritual counsel and different monasteries around the world and monastics responding to that request with a willingness to share their wisdom with others, the International Association of Lay Cistercian Communities today includes nearly fifty communities of Lay Cistercians around the world. Each community exists in association with a Cistercian monastery and typically provides spiritual formation and guidance to laypeople under the tutelage of both monastic and lay leadership.

Because community is such an important element of Cistercian spirituality, to become a Lay Cistercian requires membership with one of the Lay Cistercian communities. We do not have "solitary" or "at-large" membership. Thankfully, several communities have a strong online presence which allows people to participate even if they do not live close enough to an abbey to attend regular meetings.

Becoming a Lay Cistercian is similar to becoming a monk. It is a calling, and so the process begins with a period of discernment, when inquirers are invited to learn more about Lay Cistercian spirituality and community. It's an invitation to reflect on whether this unique expression of Christian discipleship might be right for them. The purpose behind being a Lay Cistercian is to grow as followers of Jesus Christ, and we recognize that many different paths exist for those who are seeking a closer walk with Christ. Cistercian spirituality represents just one such path.

For those who do feel so called, membership in their local Lay Cistercian community typically involves a period of formation, in which the newcomer learns about the community and the way of life that Cistercian spirituality entails. The length of this formation period and the requirements for it vary from community to community. Eventually, once one has completed the formation process, the new Lay Cistercian has the opportunity to make lifetime promises to both the Lay Cistercian community and its sponsoring monastery. Making life promises is a joyful occasion that marks not the end but a transition in a Lay Cistercian's formation. Once the vows are professed, the journey continues; seeking to grow in grace and holiness is a lifelong commitment.

What do Lay Cistercians do? Again, specific requirements vary according to local customs, but many Lay Cistercian communities expect that their members will be committed followers of Jesus Christ who pray daily, incorporating lectio divina, the Divine Office, and silent contemplation into their daily practice. Most Lay Cistercian groups have monthly gathering days and an annual retreat. Lay Cistercians are also encouraged to meet regularly with a spiritual director and to contribute to the welfare of the monastery both through financial gifts and volunteer efforts. Some Lay Cistercian communities restrict their membership to practicing Roman Catholics, but others welcome Christians of all denominations.

There are many blessings in the Lay Cistercian way of life; what I personally find so rewarding is simply the opportunity to participate in a community where the members share my love for contemplation, prayer, and the wisdom found in monastic expressions of faith. Knowing that this community exists and that I am a part of it is a great motivation and support for me as I live my day-to-day life, especially as I seek to remain faithful to the daily demands of prayer and silence.

If you think the Lay Cistercian path might be for you, you can learn more about it (and find the name and contact information of the Lay Cistercian community closest to you) by visiting cistercianfamily.org.

CONTEMPLATIVE OUTREACH:
A MINISTRY WITH CISTERCIAN ROOTS

One of the most visible ministries to emerge out of the Cistercian world in recent decades is the centering prayer movement. Centering prayer is a form of silent meditation that is anchored in ancient Christian teachings, such as the writings of John Cassian from the fifth century and *The Cloud of Unknowing,* written in the fourteenth century. As a method of praying, centering prayer was developed by several monks of Saint Joseph's Abbey in Spencer, Massachusetts, in the 1970s; after one of those monks, M. Basil Pennington, wrote an influential book on the topic, *Centering Prayer: Renewing an Ancient Christian Prayer Form,* the practice became popular and Contemplative Outreach was formed in 1983 to support centering prayer practitioners. On the surface, the ministry of Contemplative Outreach and the practice of centering prayer may not seem particularly Cistercian, mainly because the emphasis is on making silent prayer accessible to all Christians. However, the roots of this movement and its commitment to silence, simplicity, and listening for the quiet presence of God, all emerge out of the Cistercian tradition. For more information, visit contemplativeoutreach.org.

CISTERCIAN ABBEYS IN NORTH AMERICA

Cistercian monasteries can be found all over the world, and more than twenty-five such communities are currently in the United States and Canada. The following list provides addresses and websites for the North American monasteries, noting which communities are men and which are women as well as which follow the common or strict observance. Some monasteries choose not to manage a website, so if no website is listed, none is currently available as of when this list was compiled.

CISTERCIAN MONASTERIES IN THE UNITED STATES

Abbey of Gethsemani (strict observance, men)
3642 Monks Road
Trappist, KY 40051-6152
www.monks.org

Abbey of New Clairvaux (strict observance, men)
P.O. Box 80
26240 Seventh Street
Vina, CA 96092-0080
www.newclairvaux.org

Abbey of Our Lady of the Holy Trinity (strict observance, men)
1250 South 9500 East
Huntsville, UT 84317
www.holytrinityabbey.org

The Abbey of the Genesee (strict observance, men)
3258 River Road
Piffard, NY 14533
www.geneseeabbey.org

Assumption Abbey (strict observance, men)
Rt 5 P.O. Box 1056
Ava, MO 65608-9120
www.assumptionabbey.org

Mepkin Abbey (strict observance, men)
1098 Mepkin Abbey Road
Moncks Corner, SC 29461-4796
www.mepkinabbey.org

Monastery of the Holy Spirit (strict observance, men)
2625 Highway 212 SW
Conyers, GA 30094-4044
www.trappist.net

Mount Saint Mary's Abbey (strict observance, women)
300 Arnold Street
Wrentham, MA 02093-1799
www.msmabbey.org

New Melleray Abbey (strict observance, men)
6632 Melleray Circle
Peosta, IA 52068-7079
www.newmelleray.org

Our Lady of Dallas Cistercian Abbey (common observance, men)
1 Cistercian Road
Irving, TX 75039-4599
www.cistercian.org

Our Lady of Fatima Monastery (common observance, men)
564 Walton Avenue
Mt. Laurel, NJ 08054-9506
www.fatimamonastery.com

Our Lady of Guadalupe Abbey (strict observance, men)
9200 NE Abbey Road
Carlton, OR 97111-9504
www.trappistabbey.org

Our Lady of the Angels Monastery (strict observance, women)
3365 Monastery Drive
Crozet, VA 22932-2116
www.olamonastery.org

Our Lady of the Holy Cross Abbey (strict observance, men)
901 Cool Spring Lane
Berryville, VA 22611-2700
www.virginiatrappists.org

Our Lady of the Mississippi Abbey (strict observance, women)
8400 Abbey Hill Road
Dubuque, IA 52003-9501
www.mississippiabbey.org

Redwoods Monastery (strict observance, women)
18104 Briceland Thorn Road
Whitethorn, CA 95589-8901
www.redwoodsabbey.org

Saint Benedict's Monastery (strict observance, men)
1012 Monastery Road
Snowmass, CO 81654-9399
www.snowmass.org

Saint Joseph's Abbey (strict observance, men)
167 North Spencer Road
Spencer, MA 01562-1233
www.spencerabbey.org

Santa Rita Abbey (strict observance, women)
14200 E. Fish Canyon Road
Sonoita, AZ 85637-6545
www.santaritaabbey.org

Valley of Our Lady Monastery (common observance, women)
E11096 Yanke Drive
Prairie du Sac, WI 53578-9737
www.nunocist.org

CISTERCIAN MONASTERIES IN CANADA

Abbaye Notre-Dame du Bon Conseil (strict observance, women)
670 Rang Sainte-Évelyne
Saint-Benoît-Labre, Québec G0M 1P0

Abbaye Val Notre-Dame (strict observance, men)
250, Chemin de la Montagne Coupée
Saint-Jean-de-Matha, Québec J0K 2S0
www.abbayevalnotredame.ca

Monastère Notre-Dame de Mistassini (strict observance, men)
100 Route des Trappistes
Dolbeau-Mistassini, Québec G8L 5E5
www.monasteremistassini.org

Notre-Dame de l'Assomption Abbay (strict observance, women)
CP 1010
Rogersville, New Brunswick, E4Y 2W8
www.trappistine.org

Our Lady of Calvary Abbey (strict observance, men)
11505 Route 126
Rogersville, New Brunswick E4Y 2N9
www.calvaryabbey.com

Our Lady of the Prairies Abbey (strict observance, men)
PO Box 310
Holland, Manitoba R0G 0X0

RETREATS AND GUEST HOUSE INFORMATION

"All guests who present themselves are to be welcomed as Christ," wrote Saint Benedict in his holy *Rule,* instructing monks and nuns to make hospitality an essential part of their intentional Christian life. To this day, nearly all monasteries of the Benedictine tradition, including the Cistercians, recognize that receiving guests is a central and joyful part of their life as monastics. Visitors are welcome for a brief visit of a few hours, a several-day retreat, and in some locations, even for longer stays. Generally speaking, a *visitor* or *guest* refers to someone who comes to a monastery without necessarily seeking to become a nun or monk. Married guests and non-Catholic guests are welcomed along with those who might be more specifically discerning if they are being called to monastic life.

A few monasteries have large guest houses and offer conferences or retreats structured around a specific theme. Many others offer no such programming but rather create the space where visitors may enter into the silence and prayer of the monastic community, a place where one may seek to encounter God. In some locations, guests can participate in the daily work of the monastic community. However, it's important to remember that all monasteries have cloistered areas that are off-limits to guests and visitors. This is to preserve the contemplative character of the abbey, as well as to protect the privacy of the monastics.

If you wish to visit a monastery or make a retreat (and I hope you do), visit the website of an abbey near you, and look for "guest," "visitor" or "retreat" information. There you will find details on how to reserve your room, the cost or suggested donation, and other pertinent information.

MONK PRODUCTS: FRUITCAKE, PRESERVES, FUDGE, AND MORE

While in the popular imagination nuns and monks are holy people who devote endless hours to meditation and contemplation, in reality they are down-to-earth folks who have to make a living just like everyone else. Saint Benedict's emphasis on labor as an important characteristic of monastic life is not about busywork but rather indicates how every community has one or more business or industry, ways that the monks and nuns collectively earn their keep.

Many monasteries are renowned for a variety of food products—from bread to cheese to mushrooms to candy to fruitcakes. Others make religious supplies such as incense, stained glass, rosaries, or communion bread. A few have other income streams ranging from bonsai to bookbinding to handmade caskets and cremation urns. Most monasteries have a gift shop where you can purchase products made by the monks (or by employees under their guidance). Others sell their wares through their websites. Visit the following sites to explore the variety of goods you can purchase from monks—a great way to support this centuries-old way of life.

Trappistine Quality Candy
The Trappistine nuns of Wrentham, Massachusetts, offer crunch and chocolate candies.
www.trappistinecandy.com

Monastery Candy
Caramels, mints, and truffles are made by the nuns of Our Lady of the Mississippi Abbey.
www.monasterycandy.com

Trappist Preserves
A large selection of jams, preserves, and marmalades are made by the monks of Spencer, Massachusetts.
www.trappistpreserves.com

Spencer Trappist Ale
Traditionally, "Trappist ale" referred only to beer from a small number of monasteries in Belgium. But Saint Joseph's Abbey in the Unites Stated has launched its own microbrewery, featuring the only certified Trappist beer made in the country.
www.spencerbrewery.com

Trappist Caskets
The monks of New Melleray Abbey in Iowa prayerfully make these beautifully handcrafted cremation urns and caskets.
www.trappistcaskets.com

Gethsemani Farms
This site features cheese, fruitcake, and fudge (made with real Kentucky bourbon) from Gethsemani Abbey.
www.gethsemanifarms.org

Monks' Bread
Genesee Abbey in New York sells its own monk-made bread along with a variety of other delicious products (including monk-made honey and preserves) on this website.
www.monksbread.com

Holy Spirit Monastery Gifts
Holy Spirit Abbey in Georgia offers a selection of fruitcakes, fudge, biscotti, and other tasty treats.
www.holyspiritmonasterygifts.com

Honey Creek Woodlands
This natural cemetery is owned and operated by the monks of Georgia on forested monastery land.
www.honeycreekwoodlands.com

Monastery Fruitcake
The monks of Holy Cross Abbey in Virginia are renowned for their creamed honey; this site features fruitcake, honey, and truffles for sale.
www.monasteryfruitcake.org

NOTES

INTRODUCTION

1. Quoted in John Kiser, *The Monks of Tibhirine: Faith, Love, and Terror in Algeria* (New York: Saint Martin's Press, 2003), 146.

2. Monks of the Cistercian Order of the Strict Observance, (Constitutions 2005), 1:3.5.

3. Other translations call this the "still small voice" of God (KJV) or even "a light silent sound" (NABRE).

1. Charism

1. Thomas Merton, *Conjectures of a Guilty Bystander* (New York: Image Books, 2009), 153–154.

2. Ibid.

2. Sacred Stories

1. Michael Casey, *Fully Human, Fully Divine: An Interactive Christology* (Liguori, MO: Liguori/Triumph, 2004), Kindle edition, locations 217–221.

2. Sermon preached by Father Anthony Delisi at the Lay Cistercian Gathering Day, Conyers, GA, December 2, 2007.

3. Formation

1. Eric Schlosser, *Fast Food Nation: The Dark Side of the All-American Meal* (New York: Mariner Books, 2012), 59–90, 239–243.

2. "Statement on the Formation of Lay Cistercians," June 20, 2014, accessed October 7, 2014, http://www.cistercianfamily.org/documents/Formation%20 Declaration-FINAL-20June2014.pdf.

3. Mette Birkedal Bruun, *The Cambridge Companion to the Cistercian Order* (Cambridge: Cambridge University Press, 2014), Kindle edition, locations 5639–5640. See also Bernard of Clairvaux's *Sermons on the Song of Songs*, 3, 4, 6–9.

4. Humility

1. Michael Casey, *A Guide to Living in the Truth: Saint Benedict's Teachings on Humility* (Liguori, MO: Liguori Publications, 2001).

2. Bernard of Clairvaux, "On the Steps of Humility and Pride," in *Bernard of Clairvaux: Selected Works*, trans. Gillian R. Evans (New York: Paulist Press, 1987), 116.

3. Michael Casey, *A Guide to Living in the Truth* (Liguori, MO: Liguori Publications, 2001), Kindle edition, locations 62–78

4. Ibid.

5. Hospitality

1. Thomas Merton, *The Waters of Siloe* (Orlando, FL: Harvest/HBJ Book, 1979), Kindle edition, location 1889.

6. Compassion and Community

1. International Association of Lay Cistercian Communities, "The Lay Cistercian Spiritual Journey," June 20, 2014, http://www.cistercianfamily.org/documents/Spiritual%20Journey%20FINAL%2020June2014.pdf

2. Wendell Berry, *Sex, Economy, Freedom and Community* (New York: Pantheon Books, 1993), 119–120.

3. Thomas Merton, *Cistercian Life* (Cistercian Book Service, 1974), 49.

4. Santiago Fidel Ordóñez, foreword to *The Sun at Midnight*, by Bernardo Olivera (Collegeville, MN: Cistercian Publications, 2012), ix.

5. Gilbert of Hoyland, quoted in *The Way of Simplicity*, by Esther de Waal (London: Darton, Longman and Todd, 1998), 155.

6. *The Rule of Saint Benedict*, prologue 49.

7. Prayer and Liturgy

1. Gilbert of Hoyland, "Sermon 15," quoted in Jean Holman, "Monastic Joyfulness in Gilbert of Hoyland," *Cistercian Studies Quarterly* 19 (1984.4), 331.

2. Guerric of Igny, "Sermon 22:5," quoted in M. Basil Pennington, *A School of Love: The Cistercian Way to Holiness* (Norwich: Canterbury Press, 2000), 78.

3. Augustine Roberts, *Finding the Treasure* (Collegeville, MN: Liturgical Press, 2011), Kindle edition, location 1418.

4. Ibid., location 1372.

5. Guerric of Igny, "Sermon 54:5," in Pennington, *School of Love* 78–79.

8. Contemplation

1. Merton, *Waters of Siloe*, 278.

2. *Catechism of the Catholic Church*, 2nd ed. (Vatican: Libreria Editrice Vaticana, 1997), 872.

3. See "Mind Monkey," http://en.wikipedia.org/wiki/Mind_monkey (accessed April 2, 2015); Martin Laird, *Into the Silent Land: A Guide to the Christian Practice of Contemplation* (Oxford: Oxford University Press, 2006), especially 4, 15, 20, 77.

4. Bernard of Clairvaux, *Homilies in Praise of the Blessed Virgin Mary*, trans. Marie-Bernard Saïd (Kalamazoo, MI: Cistercian Publications, 1993), 30–31.

5. Bernardo Olivera, O.C.S.O., *The Sun at Midnight*, trans. Augustine Roberts, O.C.S.O. (Collegeville, MN: Cistercian Publications, 2012), 12.

6. Quoted in Pauline Matarasso, ed., *The Cistercian World* (London: Penguin Books, 1993), Kindle edition, locations 134–135.

7. Thomas Keating, *Open Mind, Open Heart: The Contemplative Dimension of the Gospel* (New York: Continuum, 1996), 98.

8. Agnes Day, O.C.S.O., *Light in the Shoe Shop: A Cobbler's Contemplations* (Kalamazoo, MI: Cistercian Publications, 2013), Kindle edition, location 1599.

9. Keating, *Open Mind, Open Heart*, 10–11.

10. Thomas Merton, *Thoughts in Solitude* (New York: Farrar, Straus and Cudahy, 1958), 83.

11. Keating, *Open Mind, Open Heart*, 11.

9. Conversion of Life

1. Francis Kline, O.C.S.O., *Four Ways of Holiness for the Universal Church: Drawn from the Monastic Tradition* (Collegeville, MN: Cistercian Publications, 2007).

2. Berry, *Sex, Economy, Freedom and Community*, 110–111.

3. Henri Nouwen, *The Genesee Diary* (New York: Doubleday, 1976), Kindle edition, locations 1586–1589

4. Keating, *Open Mind, Open Heart*.

5. Michael Casey, "Bernard's Biblical Mysticism," *Studies in Spirituality* 4, (1994): 12–30.

10. Stability

1. Beatrice of Nazareth, "The Seven Manners of Holy Love," in *The Life of Beatrice of Nazareth*, trans. Roger DeGanck (Kalamazoo, MI: Cistercian Publications, 1991), 289–331.

2. Ibid.

3. Merton, *Waters of Siloe*.

4. See Veronica Rolf, *Julian's Gospel*, Kindle edition, location 3923, for more information on affective devotion as taught by the Cistercian fathers.

11. Perseverance

1. To order it (directly from the sisters) go to http://www.monasterycandy.com/Detail?prod=62.

2. Nouwen, *Genesee Diary*, Kindle edition, location 2673.

3. M. Basil Pennington, O.C.S.O., *The Cistercians* (Collegeville, MN: Liturgical Press, 1992), 77.

4. "Statement on the Formation of Lay Cistercians," June 20, 2014, accessed October 7, 2014, http://www.cistercianfamily.org/documents/Formation%20Declaration-FINAL-20June2014.pdf.

5. Casey, *Guide to Living in the Truth*, Kindle edition, locations 2613–2614.

6. Casey, *Fully Human, Fully Divine*, Kindle edition, locations 39–41.

7. Ibid.

SELECTED BIBLIOGRAPHY

Note: books marked with an asterisk (*) are particularly recommended for further reading on Cistercian spirituality.

Aelred of Rievaulx. *The Mirror of Charity*. Translated by Elizabeth Conner, O.C.S.O. Kalamazoo, MI: Cistercian Publications, 1990.

———. *Spiritual Friendship*. Commentary by Dennis Billy, C.Ss.R. Notre Dame, IN: Christian Classics, 2008.

Benedict, *RB 1980: The Rule of Saint Benedict in Latin and English with Notes*. Edited by Timothy Fry, Timothy Horner, and Imogene Baker. Collegeville, MN: Liturgical Press, 1981.

Bernard of Clairvaux. *Homilies in Praise of the Blessed Virgin Mary*. Translated by Marie-Bernard Saïd. Kalamazoo, MI: Cistercian Publications, 1993.

———. *The Letters*. Translated by Bruno Scott James. London: Burnes & Oates, 1958.

———. *Selected Works*. Translated by Gillian R. Evans. New York: Paulist Press, 1987.

Behrens, James Stephen, O.C.S.O. *Portraits of Grace: Images and Words from the Monastery of the Holy Spirit*. Skokie, IL: ACTA Publications, 2007.

Berry, Wendell. *Sex, Economy, Freedom and Community*. New York: Pantheon Books, 1993.

*Bianco, Frank. *Voices of Silence: Lives of the Trappists Today*. New York: Paragon House, 1991.

Bruun, Mette Birkedal, ed. *The Cambridge Companion to the Cistercian Order*. Cambridge: Cambridge University Press, 2013.

Casey, Michael, O.C.S.O. *Fully Human, Fully Divine: An Interactive Christology*. Liguori, MO: Liguori/Triumph, 2004.

———. *A Guide to Living in the Truth: Saint Benedict's Teaching on Humility*. Liguori, MO: Liguori/Triumph, 2001.

———. *The Road to Eternal Life: Reflections on the Prologue of Benedict's Rule*. Collegeville, MN: Liturgical Press, 2010.

———. *Sacred Reading: The Ancient Art of Lectio Divina*. Liguori, MO: Liguori/Triumph, 1996.

———. *Strangers to the City: Reflections on the Beliefs and Values of the Rule of Saint Benedict*. Brewster, MA: Paraclete Press, 2005.

———. *Toward God: The Ancient Wisdom of Western Prayer*. Liguori, MO: Liguori/ Triumph, 1996.

Cassian, John. *Conferences*. Translated by Colm Luibheid. New York: Paulist Press, 1985.

Catechism of the Catholic Church. 2nd rev. and enlarged ed. Rome: Libreria Editrice Vaticana, 2000.

Cummings, Charles, O.C.S.O. *Eco-Spirituality: Toward a Reverent Life*. Mahwah, NJ: Paulist Press, 1991.

*———. *Monastic Practices*. Kalamazoo, MI: Cistercian Publications, 1986.

Dante. *The Divine Comedy: Inferno, Purgatorio, Paradiso*. Translated by Robin Kirkpatrick. London: Penguin Books, 2012.

*Day, Agnes, O.C.S.O. *Light in the Shoe Shop: A Cobbler's Contemplations*. Collegeville, MN: Cistercian Publications, 2013.

*Day, Trisha. *Inside the School of Charity: Lessons from the Monastery*. Collegeville, MN: Cistercian Publications, 2009.

Delisi, Anthony, O.C.S.O. *Black Like Licorice*. Norcross, GA: Trinity Press, 2011.

———. *Praying in the Cellar*. Brewster, MA: Paraclete Press, 2005.

*———. *What Makes a Cistercian Monk?* Conyers, GA: Monastery of the Holy Spirit, 2003.

Derwahl, Freddy. *The Last Monk of Tibhirine*. Brewster, MA: Paraclete Press, 2013.

DeVogué, Adalbert, O.S.B. *Reading Saint Benedict: Reflections on the Rule*. Kalamazoo, MI: Cistercian Publications, 1994.

DeWaal, Esther. *The Way of Simplicity*. London: Darton, Longman and Todd, 1998.

Fitzpatrick, Gail, O.C.S.O. *Seasons of Grace*. Skokie, IL: ACTA Publications, 2000.

Francis. *Evangelii Gaudium*. Boston: Pauline Books & Media, 2013.

Keating, Thomas, O.C.S.O. *Open Mind, Open Heart: The Contemplative Dimension of the Gospel*. New York: Continuum, 1996.

Kiser, John. *The Monks of Tibhirine: Faith, Love, and Terror in Algeria*. New York: Saint Martin's Press, 2003.

Kline, Francis, O.C.S.O. *Four Ways of Holiness for the Universal Church*. Kalamazoo, MI: Cistercian Publications, 2007.

Kramer, Dewey Weiss. *Open to the Spirit: Tradition and Continuity at Holy Spirit Monastery*. Third Edition. Conyers, GA: Monastery of the Holy Spirit, 2011.

Laird, Martin, O.S.A. *Into the Silent Land: A Guide to the Christian Practice of Contemplation*. Oxford: Oxford University Press, 2006.

*Louf, André, O.C.S.O. *The Cistercian Way*. Kalamazoo, MI: Cistercian Publications, 1983.

Manss, Virginia, and Mary Frohlich, eds. *The Lay Contemplative: Testimonies, Perspectives, Resources.* Cincinnati: Saint Anthony Messenger Press, 2000.

Marechal, Elias, O.C.S.O. *Tears of an Innocent God.* Mahwah, NJ: Paulist Press, 2015.

Matarasso, Pauline, ed. *The Cistercian World: Monastic Writings of the Twelfth Century.* London: Penguin Books, 1993.

McCabe, Maureen F., O.C.S.O. *I am the Way: Stages of Prayer in Saint Bernard.* Collegeville, MN: Cistercian Publications, 2012.

McColman, Carl. *Answering the Contemplative Call.* Charlottesville, VA: Hampton Roads, 2013.

Merton, Thomas, O.C.S.O. *Cistercian Life.* Conyers, GA: Our Lady of Holy Spirit Abbey, 2001.

———. *Conjectures of a Guilty Bystander.* New York: Image Books, 2009.

———. *The Inner Experience: Notes on Contemplation.* New York: HarperCollins, 2003.

———. *New Seeds of Contemplation.* New York: New Directions, 1962.

———. *The Seven Storey Mountain.* New York: Harcourt, Brace and Company, 1948.

———. *Thoughts in Solitude.* New York: Farrar, Straus and Cudahy, 1958.

*———. *The Waters of Siloe.* Garden City, NY: Garden City Books, 1951.

———. *The Wisdom of the Desert.* New York: New Directions, 1960.

Nouwen, Henri. *The Genesee Diary: Report from a Trappist Monastery.* New York: Image Books, 1981.

Okholm, Dennis. *Monk Habits for Everyday People: Benedictine Spirituality for Protestants.* Grand Rapids, MI: Brazos Press, 2007.

Olivera, Bernardo, O.C.S.O. *How Far to Follow? The Martyrs of Atlas.* Kalamazoo, MI: Cistercian Publications, 1997.

———. *The Sun at Midnight: Monastic Experience of the Christian Mystery.* Collegeville, MN: Cistercian Publications, 2010.

Our Lady of the Mississippi Abbey. *The Monastery.* Dubuque, IA: Our Lady of the Mississippi Abbey, 2006.

Pennington, M. Basil, O.C.S.O. *A School of Love: This Cistercian Way to Holiness.* Norwich, England: The Canterbury Press, 2000.

———. *The Cistercians.* Collegeville, MN: The Liturgical Press, 1992.

Pollard, Miriam, O.C.S.O. *The Laughter of God: At Ease with Prayer.* Wilmington, DE: Michael Glazier, 1986.

*Roberts, Augustine, O.C.S.O. *Finding the Treasure: Letters from a Global Monk.* Collegeville, MN: Cistercian Publications, 2011.

Rolf, Veronica. *Julian's Gospel.* Maryknoll, NY: Orbis Books, 2013.

Sellner, Edward C. *Finding the Monk Within: Great Monastic Values for Today.* Mahwah, NJ: Hidden Spring, 2008.

*Sweeney, Jon. *Cloister Talks: Learning from My Friends the Monks.* Grand Rapids. MI: Brazos Press, 2009.

Thomas, Robert, O.C.S.O. *Passing from Self to God: A Cistercian Retreat.* Kalamazoo, MI: Cistercian Publications, 2006.

William of Saint Thierry. *On the Nature and Dignity of Love.* Kalamazoo, MI: Cistercian Publications, 1981.

Carl McColman is the author of *The Big Book of Christian Mysticism* and *Answering the Contemplative Call*, and writes for *Patheos*, *Huffington Post*, and *Contemplative Journal*. He also has his own popular website and blog devoted to Christian and world mysticism. McColman is a member of the Lay Cistercians of Our Lady of the Holy Spirit, a contemplative community under the spiritual guidance of Trappist monks. A Catholic in full-time ministry as a retreat leader and speaker, McColman frequently leads workshops and retreats on contemplative spirituality at churches, seminaries, monasteries and retreat centers.

McColman earned a bachelor's degree in English (magna cum laude) from James Madison University in 1982, and a master's in English from George Mason University in 1984. He was trained in the practice of Christian contemplation through the Shalem Institute for Spiritual Formation in Washington, DC. He received training in spiritual direction from the Institute for Pastoral Studies in Atlanta. He lives in Stone Mountain, Georgia.